TALL TALES
of
YORK COUNTY

TALL TALES
of
YORK COUNTY

GHOSTLY SECRETS, DAREDEVIL PREACHERS *and* WALKING ON WATER

JERRY L. WEST

THE
History
PRESS

Published by The History Press
Charleston, SC 29403
www.historypress.net

Cover image: William Beatty Smith of Clover. *Courtesy of the Museum of Western York County.*

First published 2006

Manufactured in the United States

ISBN-13 978.1.59629.190.4

Library of Congress Cataloging-in-Publication Data

Tall tales of York County : ghostly secrets, daredevile priests and walking
on water / [compiled by] Jerry L. West.
p. cm.
ISBN-13: 978-1-59629-190-4 (alk. paper)
ISBN-10: 1-59629-190-7 (alk. paper)
1. Tall tales--South Carolina--York County. 2. York County
(S.C.)--Folklore. I. West, Jerry Lee.
GR110.S7T35 2006
398.209757'43--dc22
2006027440

CONTENTS

CONTENTS

CONTENTS

PREFACE

Bertram Wyatt-Brown points out in his *Southern Honor* that storytelling is the oldest form of history. Since the beginning of time man has enjoyed the art of storytelling, from small dramatic events of the day to the more elaborate and complex mythologies—all giving meaning and definition to the world around. All historians—amateur and professional—would agree that historical works are no more than a string of facts arranged into story form. A few have a natural curiosity that drives them to discovering a story; all are satisfied by a story. Since it has been my joy to discover and arrange *Tall Tales of York County*, it is hoped that the reader's desire to be entertained will be fulfilled. Storytelling is an important facet to life because it connects us to history. If no one tells the stories of bygone days, then we have no connection to the past. Perhaps that is one of the problems with our modern world. The telling of such tragedies as World War I, World War II, the sinking of the Titanic, the Great Depression and the destruction of the New York World Trade Center expresses the human experience. Even the small, almost insignificant events of everyday life are important enough to be told, for they are life's simple adhesive. York County is a wonderful place to live; it is a "storied" place. It is a place filled with large and small stories that give meaning to the area and define its culture. Within the minds of its people are archived a thousand stories and they love to hear and tell them, all the while making an otherwise mundane life a bit more exciting. Pity the people who have no stories to share in their living rooms, on the street, under a shade tree near a corn field, a front porch or over the bed of an old pickup truck. York County is not one of those places; it is truly a storied place. The reader of these tall tales should not take lightly the homey image they reflect, or be deceived by their seeming insignificance, for they are filled with values that define and bind a people, and exist as art in its least pretentious form. Though they are but samples and fragments of time and events, they made a lasting impression upon those who have gone before us. These are stories of heroes who have triumphed over great odds, of simple events in simple lives, of dupes and rogues—all wonderful people who lived in York County. Some of these tales may be familiar to the reader and have an obvious conclusion, while others will leave the reader to wonder about the outcome. The original inspiration for this collection of fables, yarns and tales was friend and county historian Samuel B. Mendenhall, who published *Tales of York County* in 1989. When Sam died in 1999, the county lost one of its principle historians and storytellers. Like Sam, I relied heavily on the *Yorkville Enquirer* to gather events from earlier days; therefore, our subject matter sometimes overlaps, though we each interpret it in our own style. Other tales came from various sources, both printed and oral.

MASSACRE ON
BUFFALO CREEK

Somewhere on Buffalo Creek in what is now Cherokee County one of the bloodiest massacres on the east side of the Broad River occurred. In the summer of 1754 a wagon train of settlers was winding down the Broad River basin toward the King's Creek area. The small caravan stopped at the home of a Mr. Autry, who was known for receiving and welcoming travelers. At that time, a young Goforth man and his fiancée decided to leave the group to seek a minister to get married. Sometime after the event, on October 7, 1754, Captain James Francis wrote to Governor Glenn of South Carolina reporting the particulars of the savage attack:

May it please your excellency, I should have written sooner concerning this cruel murder, perpetrated, as I suppose, by a camp of French Indians, if I had not heard that Mr. Wilcox of this neighborhood had already set off for town to inform you of the same. On a stream called Buffalo creek, supposed by some to be in North Carolina, and by others, in the southern province, at the house of a Mr. Outtery, a sociable, hospitable man, and of good resolution, where several families, traveling from the north, had put up; at the same unfortunate time a family from the neighborhood had also come in to wait the return of a young couple, who had gone some forty or more miles to a Justice of the Peace to be married. In the meantime a party of sixty Indians came upon these unhappy people, twenty-one in all, and murdered sixteen of them on the spot. Their bodies were found scattered around in a circumference of some two or three hundred yards, the remaining five were either carried off or killed at a distance from the place where they were attacked. They had not yet been heard from; among them are a woman and three children—of the fifth one I could get no account. This sir is the exact story of this unhappy affair, as far as it relates to the murdered people. Immediately after dispatching these, the savages killed all the hogs, fowls and cattle about the premises and heaped their carcasses upon the dead bodies of the men and women. Twenty head of horses, some of them very valuable, which had belonged to the travelers, were driven off. But a single one of the butchered people fell by a gunshot; the rest were all killed by means of arrows and tomahawks, many of which were found sticking in their bodies. The first who discovered the bloody deed were the newly married couple, who returned soon after it was all over, and the Indians just gone. They were completely panic stricken but stayed long enough to bury the dead, by throwing them hurriedly into a well, which was, near the house.

Buffalo Creek is about five miles from where the path crosses Broad River, that leads from the Cherokees to the Catawbas and Outtery's plantation some twenty miles from that ford which is one hundred miles from the Saluda settlement.

The governor made serious efforts to recover the captured children. Even a year later he was writing a trader in the King's Creek region enlisting his help to rescue a child from a party of Savannahs that might have been one of the kidnapped. A short time later he received a letter from John Elliott of Choate informing him that when a party of Savannahs came to his place they had two white children with them. When they were asked about the children they claimed that they had obtained them from those who committed the massacre at Buffalo Creek. Elliott made a desperate attempt to get the children from the party, but was unsuccessful, and the children were never heard of after that.

I WANT TO BE KILLED BY
A GENTLEMAN

During antebellum days Abram Smith owned about three thousand acres on Guyon Moore Creek, but took little interest in the farm and usually let his slaves do as they pleased. One old slave, Jack, was a kind of foreman and worked himself and the other slaves as he saw fit. Jack's haphazard management made very little money for himself or his owner. One Saturday afternoon a neighbor and successful farmer, James Scoggins, came by the field where Jack was plowing and saw that the spaces between the furrows were eight feet wide rather than the usual two. Scoggins asked Jack what was he was planting. "Corn," he said. "Then why are you laying out the rows so far apart?" asked Scoggins. "Cause I want to get done soon!" responded Jack.

James L. Strain. *Courtesy of the Museum of Western York County.*

A few years later, as war clouds began to gather over South Carolina, militia units were frequently called to prepare themselves for a sudden emergency. Some men who envisioned a leading military role for themselves made efforts to form companies. Sometimes when volunteers were not forthcoming, these would-be captains threatened a draft. Abram grew very concerned over these threats, not fancying himself a fighting man. One day he ran into Sam Strain and expressed his concern, saying, "I don't know what they want me for, I'm no fighter. Why don't they take some of the Bolins, or Big Wash Childers, or Jack Wisher, or some of them Martins up the river? They'll all fight." Strain reminded the young man, "This is not the kind of fighting they are use to." "Well, I ain't use to it either!" snapped Smith.

"But you are slim and active and you'd be hard to hit. General Chestnut says that the Yankees can't shoot."

"Shoot, the Devil! They make the guns and you know they can use 'em!"

"But those who make guns will not be there; they will be needed in the shops. The Yankees will send their men that they have no other use for but for you to shoot at."

"That's what I hate," said Smith. "If I must be killed, I want to be killed by a gentleman!"

THE TWO JOE ROBINSONS

As the struggle for freedom arrived in the South Carolina Upcountry, the majority of the people had already chosen their sides. Sometimes these choices politically divided allegiances of families. In the Robinson family of York County, uncle and nephew, both named Joseph, found themselves in conflict. There was only about five years' difference in their ages, but they were light years apart in their ideologies. Before the beginning of the conflict, the elder Robinson had served as a major in the New Acquisition militia, but when war was declared he threw his lot with the king and was placed in command of two thousand Loyalists. Robinson was sent to Ninety Six to squelch the Patriot movement. Though he was successful, when the Patriots took Charleston and drove out the last royal governor, Robinson and his men were left stranded without orders or support. The army disbanded and Major Robinson and some others fled to Florida to escape retaliation from the Patriots and to await further orders. Eventually those orders came. Robinson the elder was commissioned lieutenant colonel and formed a regiment of Carolina refugees called "The South Carolina Royalists." Not long after his return the

Bullock's Creek Presbyterian 1860 Sanctuary. *Courtesy of the Museum of Western York County.*

Patriots captured Colonel Robinson. In the fracas he was able to escape, but his home, along with an extensive library, was burned to the ground. His family barely escaped with their lives.

Joseph Robinson, the nephew, also had his troubles. On one occasion, while he was at home on leave, Tory Colonel Mayfield sent a detachment to dispose of Robinson and other Patriots they might run across. During this foray they recaptured Robert Wilson. Wilson enlisted at his father's home in 1775 and participated in the Snow Campaign and the Florida Expedition. During the siege of Charleston he was captured and sent to Haddrell's Point to nurse the sick; from there he escaped and fled to his father's home in Chester County. On June 15, 1780, a few days after Wilson reached his home, Mayfield's Tories arrived in the area, seeking out Joseph Robinson and other Patriots. In their search, Wilson was recaptured. Knowing his fate was sealed, he pretended to be willing to switch over to the King's Army, saying, "If a man can spin, he can learn to turn." He told the Tories that he would join them if he could join the cavalry, because he was tired of being in the infantry. He was offered a horse and accoutrements, but said he had a good horse and arms of his own and that he would meet them the next morning at eight o'clock at a crossroad. The Tories were agreeable and left Wilson to continue with their search for Robinson. As they rode away, Wilson, still feigning his loyalty, exclaimed, "Kill Joe Robinson! You'll have to ride fast to do that; it is nearly sundown and he lives a good bit of a way from here." Believing what Wilson said, they decided to bed down for the night and continue their search the next morning. Wilson slipped away in the darkness and gave warning to Robinson. By the time the Tories arrived at Robinson's the next morning, he and Wilson were in the camp of General Sumter. Like his uncle, Joe Robinson had participated in the prewar Snow Campaign in 1775 and the Florida Campaign in 1776. When war was proclaimed, he took part in the Briar Creek expedition under General Ashe. During the war he became known as a fighting man, serving in the battles of Hanging Rock, Fishdam Ford, Blackstock's Plantation and Williamson's Plantation, or Huck's Defeat. After the war Patriot Robinson returned to his home in the Bullock's Creek area and lived in peace until his death in 1829. His uncle, however, had all his property confiscated and he fled to British-held West Florida and then to Jamaica. Later he moved to Prince Edward Island, Canada, where he was elected to the assembly and served as an associate justice of the Supreme Court—forever loyal to the king.

FOR THE FINEST TOWN IN OLD KAINTUCK

The story goes that the little York County village of Bowling Green, located just one-half mile from the North–South Carolina line, got its name from a traveling horse trader who came to the area just before the turn of the twentieth century. This trader came over the Blue Ridge Mountains with a string of fine horses and made an overnight stop where a village would later appear. That night, he met a man from the area and, having been so impressed with the scenery, he inquired, "What do you call this section?" The resident told him it did not have a name. "Well then," questioned the horse trader, "why not name it Bowling Green for the finest town in old Kaintuck?"

JAMES MEEK REVOLUTIONARY WAR SOLDIER

James Meek came to York County Backcountry with his widowed mother from Pennsylvania. When the war with Britain began, Meek enlisted into the army of General Sumter and participated in all the general's battles, as well as the disastrous defeat at Fishing Creek. Shortly after this battle, with most of Sumter's army scattered, Meek and a number of Patriots were finding their way home when a squad of Tories under the command of Captain Mayfield attacked them. Meek was captured and, with his hands tied behind his back, was marched to Mayfield's home across the Broad River in what would become Union County. When they arrived at the river they could not find a boat, so they commandeered a hog trough and ferried their prisoner across. The Mayfield home was used as a headquarters for local Tories. Mayfield's wife, however, was a staunch Whig who secretly worked for the American cause. About noon, when the band arrived with their prisoner in tow, Mrs. Mayfield acted indifferently, but quietly prepared a hasty dinner for the Tories while they racked their weapons and posted a sentinel. She got word to her neighbor, Charley Crane, that Meek was being held prisoner at the Mayfield home and no good was expected to come of it. The Tories were awakened from their nap when a shout went up, "Yonder comes Sumter's men!" The men leaped from their slumber and ran out of the house into the surrounding woods, leaving their arms stacked in the yard. The prisoner was released and returned to camp with his compatriots. Many years after the war, James Meek headed to Alabama to attend land sales at Cahawba. Reaching the Seneca River, he spent the night in a private home. The next morning he continued his journey, but within a short time his riderless horse returned to the house. Meek could not be found and after several days of searching for his body, it was discovered among some driftwood below the ford on Seneca River. His purse was missing and it was assumed he was robbed and drowned by his attackers. He was buried on a nearby plantation.

RUN OFF FOR HIS POLITICS

The 1787 ratification of the United States Constitution had a hard row to hoe in upstate South Carolina. Most of the people of the Piedmont were Whigs who preferred life without the interference of government, especially from one that was so many miles away. The tyrannical British government had just been defeated and these Scots-Irish were definitely anti-nationalists. Although all four of the York County representatives to the 1787 convention in Philadelphia signed the Constitution, it was a different matter at home. The Ratification Convention was held in Charleston. Representing York County were William Hill, Andrew Love, Robert Patton, Samuel Watson, James Martin, James G. Hunt, Samuel Lowery, John McCaw, Adam Meek, Abraham Smith and one minister, Reverend Francis Cummings, the pastor of the Bethel Presbyterian Church. On the strength of the Lowcountry representatives the Constitution was ratified on May 23 by a vote of 149 to 73. Although outnumbered by population and representation, the Upcountry voted their convictions against a federal government. All but one of the eleven York County representatives voted against ratification. Reverend Francis Cummings voted for ratification. What made bad matters worse was that on the day before the vote Cummings and Hill had served on the same committee to draft proposals to be sent to the United States Congress for consideration as amendments. Cummings had been holding out for inclusion

Bethel Presbyterian Church. *Courtesy of the Museum of Western York County.*

of a freedom of religion clause, but some of the Federalists convinced him that the constitution secured that right with specific wording. When the constitution came up for a vote Cummings surprised his fellow delegates by switching his vote from the Whig position to that of the Federalists. His fellow representatives raised a number of eyebrows at his decision, but Hill and Watson, both members of his congregation, raised more than eyebrows. Upon his return to his congregation Cummings received an uneasy reception and had to contend with cold eyes and hot words. Within a short time, his congregation placed charges against him before the Bethel Presbytery when it ironically met at the Bethel Church. Here, within his own church, Cummings had to face charges and eventually expulsion. These charges could easily have been disposed of by the church's board of elders had they been so minded; but it seemed that Hill and Watson preferred a public statement. Cummings was charged with unlawfully depriving members of the "privileges of the church," accusing members of the "sin of sacrilege" and reminding them on the Sabbath to pay their portion of his salary.

Although the Presbytery found the charges against Cummings to be ungrounded, even as one might suspect, the congregation was determined to rid themselves of the man. Until they could come up with a plan, the congregation continued to give him the cold shoulder and then took up the oldest form of expulsion: to starve him out. Before 1789 closed, Cummings resigned and moved to Georgia.

THE FALLING DOWN EXERCISE

About 1802 Reverend Walker of Bethesda Presbyterian Church heard of a religious revival that was taking place in Kentucky and the strange phenomenon called "the falling down exercise." The value of this marvel was being discussed and debated by many of the old-school preachers and Walker decided to travel to Kentucky and see it firsthand and draw his own conclusions. Soon after his return to South Carolina he preached at a camp meeting in the Waxhaws, where he told his audience about his visit to Kentucky. With approval he told how whole congregations were "struck down by the Spirit of God, and falling confessed their sins and praised the eternal Father." Upon hearing Walker describe the phenomenon as a mighty manifestation of the presence of God, the congregation was moved and it was there that the "falling down exercise" was first seen in South Carolina. Not long after that, Walker conducted a camp meeting at his own church

People line the street of Clover for a parade, circa 1925. *Courtesy of the Museum of Western York County.*

and there many fell to the ground claiming they had been moved by the power of God. Many, however, saw the experience as "a nervous affectation, arising from sympathy and undue excitement of feeling." George Dale believed the thing was of the Devil and on more than one occasion when he witnessed the crowds writhing and groaning on the ground, he hid behind a tree and cried out, "What morose noise is this, I hear? Methinks 'tis some demoniac!" Then he ran away as though he were fleeing from a contagious disease. Others said it was the Holy Spirit. Many drunks were reformed, the profane became godly and scoffers of the Bible became true believers. One of these was Francis Ervin. He attended the camp meeting at Bethesda and experienced firsthand "the falling down exercise." Ten years later he told a friend that from that day on, he never doubted his conversion for one moment. Others who were affected by the experience fell by the wayside and returned to their sins "like a dog to his vomit." Whether it was a move of the Spirit of God or mass hysteria, "the falling down exercise" proceeded from Bethesda and spread over York County and the state "like a mighty wind stirring up dead men's bones, then lulled as a storm exhausted of its strength."

GOOD TIMES ON THE ROAD TO CHARLESTON

Prior to the Revolution and for some years afterward, the people of the Backcountry did their trading in Charleston. They wagoned or carted their goods and drove their cattle and poultry to the markets in what was then the state capital. The round trip took about a month and was filled with dangers. Neighbors would usually travel in a caravan to ward off robbers who lurked along the desolate stretches of road. On the way, a number of people with various kinds of vehicles joined the caravan. A good supply of whiskey was always handy. Around the campfires the travelers visited over the jug, cracked jokes, discussed the affairs of church and state and played pranks. Of course, the evening was not complete without a fistfight or two. Captain James Henry told that on a return trip from Charleston, he and some others stopped at what is now York and camped overnight. The next morning he lit out on foot and told the others to follow and that by the time they arrived at his home, he would have breakfast waiting for them. On his way he met up with three men heading to Charleston. Henry had never seen these men before, nor did he know they had agreed they would have some fun along the way by either running every man off or making him take a whipping. When Henry was given the challenge, he told them he was not in the habit of running or taking a whipping. Family tradition says that Jim Henry thoroughly thrashed one man and drove the others away. But there is a second version that is not quite so flattering to Captain Henry. Supposedly he was on his way back from Charleston when he met a wagon not far from York. The driver was a large man who was well advanced in years. Henry challenged the old man, saying, "I have been to Charleston and am nearly home again, and I have not had a fight yet. Get down, sir, I am determined to have a fight before I get home." The old man protested, saying, "I'm too old to fight; you must let me off." About this time, the son of the old man arrived and without any provocation, he declared he was willing to fight. Both stripped and went at it hand over fist as though they had been enemies for years. Big Jim Henry said he never learned the man's name, but would never forgot the sound thrashing he got that day.

MULE TALES

It was once told that a farmer paid a veterinarian fifteen dollars for saving the life of his mule, and did so gladly without the slightest hesitation, but raised a terrible ruckus when a physician charged him ten dollars to treat his wife for acute pneumonia. We would like to think this was a joke that only illustrates the importance of mules to the farmer.

Rufus Estes, who lived on the township line of Broad River and Bullock's Creek, owned a forty-year-old mule named Queen in 1937. The mule was known for her strength and endurance and was the subject of many discussions. Estes said he knew the exact date of his mule's birth, since he had helped foal her, and County Commissioner Howell said he recalled seeing the mule in 1902. A neighbor recalled a foxhunt when Queen demonstrated her stamina. The man said that on that hunt he rode his horse for thirty-four miles over the hills and hollows, and that Estes and the aging mule kept up the chase and even surpassed the man's fine horse.

There were always reports of mules having strange habits and quirks. One farmer in Chester County said he owned a field where a man had been murdered.

The farmer claimed that on certain occasions while plowing, his mule would balk at the exact spot of the murder, turn away and pull the plow and plowman away from the spot. It would then sit down like a dog and bray like a jackass. The story got even more eerie when the farmer purchased a new mule that had never been in that field: the mule did the exact same thing the first time he plowed the field.

A funny story was told about a mule that ate too high on the hog in Sharon shortly after World War II. Several young men, Herschel Brown, Arthur Erwin and Eugene Warmoth, were loafing around when Irby McGill stopped his truck in town on his way to a glue factory with an old broken-down mule. The three became curious about the pitiful old beast and asked McGill about his bony load. When he told them the mule was taking his last ride, they were moved with compassion and asked what he would take for the bag of bones. McGill told them he figured he could get five dollars at the processing plant and if they wanted him at that price they could make a deal. The three congratulated themselves on such a savvy deal, unaware that their investment would take them to a bargaining table where they would square off with Sharon's foremost entrepreneur, W.L. Hill. At one time Hill was said to be the county's "Dean of Merchants," known for turning a fast buck by seizing every situation where a profit might be made. The young men settled their steed in the pastures of Erwin's father. After a few days with the Erwin family, the mule checked out without leaving a forwarding address, apparently seeking room and board more to his liking. Weeks went by without a sign of the mule before they discovered that he had taken up with folks of his own kind at the barn lot of W.L. Hill. Thinking they could simply reclaim their property with a howdy-do and thank you very much, they were quickly told by the clever old merchant that the mule had run up a tab and it had to be settled before they could take ownership. When they asked how much they owed, Hill tabulated the bill at fifteen dollars. Apparently the five-dollar mule had been living high on the hog without any regard to his responsibility. The three would-be stockbrokers glanced at each other, knowing Hill had them. There was nothing to do but to offer the mule for payment. Hill agreed and the three young men walked off, thinking they had done well. Hill did not do too badly either; he sent the old mule out to one of his farms just in time for summer plowing, and it was said that the old mule brought in a good crop that fall.

THE APPARITION OF BULLOCK'S CREEK

The belief in spiritual phenomena must have been more prevalent among the earlier folk than we would like to think. It seems that things like ghosts, spooks, haunts and apparitions occupied the minds of our ancestors a great deal. Not only would the subject sometimes bother an individual, but also it would affect whole communities from time to time. Such is our tale that took place sometime after Adam Meek had been elected sheriff of York County. Toward the end of the eighteenth century, Meek, who had been described as "a man of greatest integrity, fearless in his discharge of duty and particularly distinguished for his common sense," was elected as sheriff of York County. Sometime after the election, local residents in one area of the county began being bothered by the appearance of a ghost or apparition in Gordon's old field. It was told that it was always seen near dusk along a road by the field and when it appeared it would follow a person until it reached the edge of the woods and would then disappear as suddenly as it had appeared.

As time went by the encounters became more frequent and the people grew very edgy and uneasy. They called upon the sheriff to see what he could do about this ghost and hopefully rid the area of it. Sheriff Meek began his investigation by questioning the witnesses. Early on it was obvious to the sheriff that many men he questioned were laughing off the idea of a field-haunting ghost to conceal their fears. However, one man made no bones about his fears, and when he was questioned by Meek whether he had ever heard the apparition say anything, he exclaimed, "I didn't wait for it to speak, I whipped my horse until we made it into the woods and the apparition gave up the chase!" Meek was determined to get to the root of this mystery and meet this thing that kept everyone's nerves on edge.

One evening, shortly after nightfall, the sheriff crept into the haunted field and quietly waited. It wasn't long until the phantom appeared alongside of him and, as he moved down the road through the field, it traveled along with him. Meek later said that he and the ghost walked together for some two hundred yards and talked until they reached the edge of the surrounding woods. Like everyone had said, when it reached the woods, it disappeared. Other than these few remarks, the sheriff was very silent and the apparition continued to appear. Some weeks later word got out that Sheriff Meek had vanished without saying a word to his wife or children. Family and friends were worried sick over his disappearance, fearing it might have something to do with the apparition. Speculation and

Bicentennial celebration at Bullock's Creek Church. *Courtesy of the Museum of Western York County.*

rumors spread over the countryside like wildfire. Could it have stolen him away because of some secret the sheriff had found out? Would it return in the night for another victim? Every vale and dark cove along the creek was expected to yield the sheriff's bloody and mangled body, but no trace of the sheriff could be found.

Two months later, the sheriff appeared at his home no worse than before. Yet it seemed as though an aura of mystery clung to his being. Had he been where few mortals are allowed? Until his death in 1807, the sheriff never revealed his conversation with the phantom of York County and he never told where he had been for those two months. When asked, he would simply say, "I cannot tell you now—I may before I die, but that is not certain. But this I can tell you, the ghost of Gordon's old field will never be seen again. I can assure the vicinity, it has been seen for the last time." What was the secret that Adam Meek carried with him to the grave? What had the ghost told him that night? Had it given Adam the secret to how it might be exorcised? Where was he for two months? Perhaps on some ancient hill wrestling with a being of another realm, or performing some ancient ritual of cleansing? These things we can only speculate, but we do know this: Adam Meek did not lie—the phantom of York County has never been seen since, and that was a long, long time ago.

THE McGOWAN BROTHERS

Twin brothers William and John McGowan were born about 1800 in Ireland. They received an excellent education and became well-qualified physicians before coming to the Broad River Basin. Though they were quite different in personalities, neither of them ever forgot anything they read and they could instantly recall any medical treatment they had studied. "Dr. John" and "Dr. Billy" were good physicians and had a working partnership. They developed a plan in which John would run a drugstore in Pinckneyville while William would be the main practitioner. This set the profitable course. Some time later some quack of a doctor ordered a medication that John knew was dangerous in unskilled hands. A few days later the doctor asked John why he did not send his order. John replied in his native dialect, "Ah, me friend! Dot's a dangerous medicine to put in the hands of an ignorant mon."

The brothers established the partnership because "Dr. John" was outspoken, and he was also in the habit of using jawbreaker words that were beyond the education of many he served. His vocabulary frequently left the patient or caregiver completely befuddled and when he was asked what he meant, his explanation would involve equally unfamiliar words. Dr. Joseph McClure, who was about thirty years younger than the McGowan brothers, often consulted the senior practitioners while he was a mere fledging in the medical field. One day John was giving the young doctor advice from his professional experience in his usual broad vocabulary when he related how he and his brother set up their partnership. "Dr. John" told how he did the office work, compounded prescriptions and did the "kollacshins." McCluney could not understand the word, but knowing the doctor's habit of using strange words, the younger doctor decided not to appear dumb by asking. For days, however, the word kept turning over and over in his mind, but the definition would not come and his dictionaries offered no listing. Finally, after exhausting every source, he asked someone to give him the definition. One can imagine Doctor McCluney's dismay when he was told that was the Irish dialect for "collections."

God Bless You
Mr. Rainey

Living within the boundaries of Bethesda Presbyterian Church was an old man by the name of Rainey who believed he was bewitched and suffered poor health. Nearly the whole community believed Rainey was suffering from a hex cast by Balsey Fox, who lived in the "Black Jacks." For some reason, it was believed that the only way the spell on Rainey could be broken was by obtaining the benediction "May God bless you" from the old sorceress. It was certain that the old woman wouldn't give the benediction just for the asking, so some of Rainey's friends devised a plan to trick the witch into giving the cure. All the women of the area were let in on the plan to trick the old woman.

On the day the plan was to be executed, a large group of men and women assembled around the Rainey house; but Balsey Fox was not among them. Everyone stood around not knowing what to do, for the plan called for all the women to line up one by one and each place her hands on poor old man Rainey and say, "May God bless you." The tricksters assumed the old hag would be too ashamed not to participate and by pronouncing the benediction she would break the spell and end her power over the old man.

As time passed, everyone began to believe the witch had outwitted them. Colonel Edward Lacey, of Revolutionary War fame, was on the scene and was not to be outdone by a witch. He dashed off on his trusty bay to get Mrs. Fox, who did not live very far away. In due time Lacey returned with the hag riding behind him. Some of the men and women who met Lacey and his rider immediately saw that Lacey's horse was unusually laboring for breath and sweating profusely. It could not have been caused by the extra weight; the old witch scarcely weighed more than ninety pounds. They concluded that the horse was straining under the presence of an evil power.

Now that the witch had arrived, nothing prevented the plan from proceeding. The women were given a signal to ready the trap. All the women there lined up in the hall of the house where the old man was lying, and one by one they came up to his bed, laid their hands upon him and said, "May God bless you, Mr. Rainey." All eyes were on Balsey Fox, who was the last in line. Without the slightest hesitation she approached the sick man. All around, the eyes of the spectators narrowed and just a hint of a confident smile could be seen on their faces. When Balsey reached the bed on which Rainey was lying, she laid her hands on him and said, "My God bless you, Mr. Rainey." Those nearby jerked with surprise, and with dropped chins, looked at one another in amazement. The old crone had outsmarted everyone. Her god was the devil, and instead of releasing him from her spell, she strengthened it. Rainey continued in his sick and weak condition until his death.

I'll Give You Such a Whipping!

In the days before temperance societies made their appearance in York County, the appearance of whiskey was expected at every social gathering. Alcohol consumption was treated so casually that even a minister who downed a few social drinks did not warrant the lifting of an eyebrow. A man of the cloth partaking in more than a few drinks, however, was a different story. On the day that a man named Floyd was to be hanged for the murder of Chester County Sheriff Nunn, Reverend Robert Walker of the Bethesda Presbyterian Church planned to attend.

On his way to Chester he stopped by a parishioner's home and was invited in for a drink. The housewife asked Reverend Walker to stop by and give them news of the hanging on his return trip. About sundown the church member and his son were completing some farm chores when the boy looked up and saw Reverend Walker coming at a full gallop. When the horse neared the gate, it suddenly dropped into a long trot, thinking it was about to make one of its usual stops. The sudden change in gait unbalanced Walker, who nearly lost his seat. When he regained his balance he urged the horse on and spoke to the older man with a dignified "Good afternoon, Squire." Watching the preacher disappear down the road, the boy turned to his father. "Paw, Mr. Walker was drunk!" The man responded, "Let me never hear of you saying such a thing as that again, or I'll give you such a whipping as you never had in your life!"

As the day came to a close both returned to their home, where the farmer shortly called his wife into another room and shut the door. To satisfy his curiosity the boy crept near the door and heard his father tell about the obvious drunkenness of their pastor. Eventually his mother and father appeared with solemn faces.

Two days later, the Bethesda congregation heard the old preacher tearfully confess his intemperance. Sharing his sorrow with tears the members freely forgave him and he served the church without further hindrance. Following many years of being a beloved pastor of Bethesda, the aging Walker submitted his resignation to the elders of the church and preached his final sermon.

At the close of his sermon, Reverend Walker walked out of the meetinghouse and seated himself in the shade of the forest that edged the cemetery. There he asked a member if he had noticed any decline in his preaching from the time he came to pastor the church. The man assured Walker that he had seen no change and that the sermon he had just preached equaled those he had heard from him in years gone by. Walker explained that he recalled the circumstances under which Reverend Dr. Alexander resigned from the pulpit of Bullock's Creek Church. Age had sapped his abilities and impaired his usefulness and he had fallen out of favor with his congregation. Walker said at that time he was determined he would not do his congregation such an injustice.

Reverend Joseph Alexander retired in 1804. By that time his age had rendered the once fiery Patriot and preacher into a feeble, toothless old man. For some time the church elders urged him to resign, but with every fiber of strength left in his old body he clung to his ministry. Alexander's refusal naturally created bad feelings and the congregation eventually made formal complaints to the Presbytery. The process that eventually culminated in Alexander's reluctant retirement had left a lasting impression on his son-in-law, Reverend Robert Walker.

1890 Memorial to Reverend Joseph Alexander. *From the author's collection.*

YORK COUNTY'S LARGEST TREES

It was said that the largest tree ever to have grown in York County was on the lands of Leroy McGill near the Bethany community. The tree measured thirty-three feet in circumference and was still living in the 1920s, though it was hollow. In fact, about that time a local schoolteacher took her class of fifteen to see the wonder. All sixteen said they were able to stand inside the hollow tree. About 1932, when timber was being cut on the McGill tract, the tree was sold for five dollars to a filling station operator in Lincolnton, North Carolina. The enterprising man cut a long section of the tree, covered it with a roof and placed seats inside where travelers might rest and eat lunch.

Twenty years after the tree was cut down and hauled away, another tree near the Bethany community was reported in 1952 to be the county's largest. This tree, somewhat smaller than the former giant, was reported to be twenty feet around and stood on the farm of P.M. Neisler. In earlier times women washed their clothes at a nearby spring and hung their garments on its limbs to dry, and later young people ate their picnics under its spreading limbs. Over the years many people came and monogrammed the trunk with their names and initials. It was said that on an outing, schoolteacher Miss May Fowler and an undisclosed number of her students stood within its hollow trunk and that D.D. McCarter, one time York County treasurer, said he and five other possum hunters found shelter from a rain storm in the cavity.

MOSIE GABBIE

More than likely, Moses Gabbie of the Beersheba Church community would have lived out his life in obscurity had it not been for a strange event that occurred when he was a young man in his twenties. "Mosie," as he was called, was born in 1798, the youngest son of Robert W. Gabbie, and came into public view about 1820 or 1821 when he went to live with his sister, Elizabeth Burns, and her family. About the time of his arrival, he began acting very strangely and fell into a habit of keeping odd hours and complaining he had been bewitched. All day long he would lie in bed in a kind of stupor and could be aroused only when he was directly spoken to; even then he would soon fall into a catatonic state. The oddest thing, however, was that every night, between eleven and twelve o'clock, he would let out a bloodcurdling scream, leap from his bed and disappear into the night. Equally as strange, he would return at daylight with his hands and feet full of chestnut burrs.

At first, the family thought Mosie was having nightmares that would end as suddenly as they began. This was a long time in coming and in her efforts to help her younger brother, Elizabeth questioned him about his nocturnal disappearances and why he returned so worn and full of burrs. The only thing he could say was that the old crone, Mrs. Biggert, had bewitched him. In great distress and nearly in tears, he told her that the old witch rode him every night to old Violet Weston's place and there she would hitch him to a chestnut tree in front of the old house and hold him captive while witches danced the night away.

Mosie's sister and her husband, William M. Burns, devised all kinds of ways to keep him at home during the night, but all to no avail. Every night, at the fatal hour, he would give out that awful scream, bolt out of the house and be gone until daylight. Eventually they gave up trying, yielding to the belief that Mosie Gabbie was indeed bewitched. Winter came and went, then spring and summer, and it made no difference what the weather was; rain, sleet or snow, nothing deterred Mosie from his ritual. Without failure, in the dead of the night, he would give out that hideous shout, jump out of bed and be gone until dawn. The family became so accustomed to the ritual that their sleep was not disturbed for a moment. Every morning the children dutifully picked the chestnut burrs from their poor uncle's hands and feet.

While William and Elizabeth Burns gave up any attempt to constrain Mosie, they continued with their empathy and helped any way they could. Sixty-six-year-old Sam Burns, the father of William, sympathized with Mosie and often spoke to others on the problem in hopes of finding some relief for the young man. On one occasion, while talking with Colonel William Ferguson about witches, haunts and things that go bump in the night, he mentioned the plight of his son's brother-in-law. Ferguson hooted at the very idea of witchcraft and wagered Burns he could keep him at home. Burns took the challenge and told Ferguson to come to his son's home and try what he would. A time was set for the following week. That night the family went to bed as usual, leaving the two older men with Mosie. Ferguson lay down on the floor in front of the fireplace, using an overturned chair to prop up his head, and Burns lay across the foot of the bed. The men chatted on into the night and as the evening wore on, their conversation became slow and labored and their eyelids grew heavy. Only a flickering fire cast a yellow light over the room. As the flames grew low, the two old men went to sleep before they knew it. For a while the room remained still and quiet, then suddenly the room was filled with Mosie's horrible scream. Ferguson immediately jumped up from his makeshift bed, but Burns moved somewhat slower. In the dimly lit room, Ferguson saw Burns rising up from the bed and mistook him for Mosie and leaped on him, straddling him in an effort to hold him in bed. Horror-stricken, Burns thought the witch had taken hold of him and struggled to tear himself loose from his captor. In the wrestling match, both fell off the bed with Ferguson still straddling his friend. Burns made a desperate dive under the bed and before long the double mistake was discovered, but Mosie Gabbie had made his escape and was gone for the night.

Some time later, old man Burns went to Lincolnton, North Carolina, to see Dr. Brindle, a well-known "witch doctor," and spoke with him about the pitiful condition of Mosie Gabbie. Much to Burns's delight, the doctor assured him that he could cure the pathetic wretch, and returned with him to York County. Hearing that Brindle had arrived at the Burns's home to cure Mosie, a crowd assembled in the yard of the home to watch the herb doctor break the hex.

The first thing Brindle did was to give Mosie an emetic. Within a few minutes the lad was throwing up crooked pins, needles, hairpins and other small trash. As hard as it is to believe, many who witnessed the event later said they would swear on a Bible what they saw. After the emetic had thoroughly done its work, a black cat was tied to a chair. In front of the large, curious and anxious crowd, Doctor Brindle took a dead hogweed switch and hit the cat nine times. He then gave the switch to Mosie, who was told to do the same thing. For exactly nine minutes, the doctor, his patient and the crowd stood silent. Again, the doctor thrashed the cat, then Mosie and then the wait. This continued for the better part of the day, each time using an odd number and a corresponding interval.

Doctor Brindle told Mosie that the ritual would cast a spell over the witch and make her come to the house to ask for a trivial favor. When this happened he was to refuse her at first, at which time she would be compelled to stay until she got what she wanted. Once granted the favor, she would leave and the spell would be broken.

The chastising of the cat continued until late afternoon. Finally Mrs. Biggert walked into the yard. The old woman had not been in the yard for years, but as the doctor predicted she came and asked for a favor, a pitcher of buttermilk. When she was refused, she became distressed and wandered aimlessly about the yard, wringing her hands. In a little while, the doctor gave Mrs. Burns a nod to fulfill the old woman's request. When this was done Mrs. Biggert was filled with glee and merrily went home. From that hour on, Mosie Gabbie was free of his nocturnal troubles and slept in his bed all night. Mosie lived out the rest of his life in relative quietness and obscurity. He now rests peacefully with other members of his family in the Beersheba Presbyterian Church cemetery.

GOLD FEVER

By the spring of 1851 the California gold fever had spread to York County and a number of families had gone west to answer the call of fortune. Yet it was possible to find a fortune in gold much closer to home. In March 1851, the local newspaper reported that Jacob B. Moore and son were "picking up chunks and wedges of gold" weighing as much as fifteen ounces each. When the editor of the *Miscellany* broke the news, editors of other newspapers believed that the editor had a touch of the fever and perhaps was making false reports to increase circulation.

The report of chunks and wedges certainly did create excitement in York County and soon it seemed nearly everyone was digging in the old abandoned mines. By the middle of July the editor announced weightier news when he reported that one nugget of pure gold, about the size and shape of a man's foot, had been found. The nugget, it was said, "weighed twenty one and one half pounds on Morgan Martin's steelyards."

The mystique of this oversized nugget grew over the years. Due to its shape it was sometimes referred to as the "Sheephead nugget" and grew from twenty-one pounds to twenty-seven. Even the disposition of the nugget became a mystery. Some said it went to the Smithsonian Institute. First of all it seems hardly likely that a poor miner would give away his wealth just for historical purposes. Secondly, an act of Congress, initiated when the United States received a gift of $550,000 from John Smithson of England, had created the institution in August 1846. It is very doubtful that people living in a poor, sparsely populated region would have known about the Smithsonian that was no more than five years old. On December 4, 1991, museum specialist Paul W. Pohwat of the Smithsonian Division of Mineralogy responded to an inquiry about the locally famed nugget: "We do not have in our collection now, nor have we in the past, a South Carolina gold nugget [of that weight]…We do have on display a specimen from the Loftis farm, Spartanburg County, South Carolina which weighs in at a mere 17.3 gms… We obtained the piece in 1932 from a Mrs. M. Loftis through purchase."

Another tradition wrapped around the elusive Martin nugget says that Morgan Martin hired John Wylie Moss to carry the nugget to a bank in Lancaster County. If there really was a trip to Lancaster, it seems more likely it would have been taken to an assay office at the large Haile Mine, where it was assayed and sold. So the whereabouts of this nugget still remains unsolved. Maybe it was only the exaggeration of a newsman. But every few decades or so we receive word that

Meek Hope, the first mayor of Smyrna, and wife Alice. *Courtesy of the Museum of Western York County.*

some fortune hunter, who is smitten with the fever and declares he will succeed where others have failed, reopens one of the old mines. Soon, however, the fever passes and silently the bedeviled regains his senses and quietly walks away.

A Vision of Western York County

A ttorney Xerxes X. Cushman was the editor of two of York County's first newspapers, the *People's Advocate* and the *Yorkville Encyclopedia*; both preceded the *Yorkville Enquirer*, which began in 1852. In 1827, Cushman was so impressed with the tonnage of iron that was being produced in the King's Creek and Smyrna areas that he envisioned York County would become one of the top metal producers in the nation.

York County had been involved in iron production prior to the Revolution through William Hill's Iron Works, located in the north central part of the county, but more extensive foundries were established at the end of the eighteenth century in the Broad River Basin near King's Creek. At the time Cushman wrote that a hundred tons of metal from the Cowpens Furnace was ready to be shipped to Charleston. "The day is not far distance," said Cushman, "where there will be ten times the business done and the capital employed about those works."

Cushman not only envisioned a thriving iron industry in western York County, he also believed that two of its mineral springs would become tourist attractions with the right publicity. Cain Springs (later Piedmont Springs) and Sutton Springs were locally known for their excellent healing properties and were frequented by people who lived as much as one hundred or so miles away. Hugh Cain owned Cain Springs in the 1820s and had constructed at least seven small buildings for convenience of the bathers. Cushman was so convinced of the medical qualities of these waters that he was sure if someone like General Andrew Jackson, the vice-president of the United States, or the governor honored the springs with a visit they would be off and running as tourist attractions. But no such dignitary ever came and the springs are now all but forgotten.

Whiskey jug lined with wicker. *Courtesy of the Museum of Western York County.*

It's Very Small
for Its Age

Jacob B. Moore, who was born about 1787, was said to be a man who feared no one or anything. He was a powerful man with a vice-like grip that was long remembered by anyone who fell into his bony clutches. Moore was a kind and gentle man until he was drunk, and then even his closest friend might become the object of his wrath.

Moore was a wealthy man who literally threw his money away. When he got on one of his drinking bouts he would throw about gold coins just to see his friends and acquaintances scramble on the ground. Some who knew him believed he threw thousands away. Jacob Moore certainly was a character. He rode a mare called Jenny Lind and carried a walking stick called Cephas. He had no time for church services but he, Jenny Lind and Cephas attended every public gathering where a crowd and whiskey could be found. Moore liked attention and was fond of creating a show for those around him. Sometimes he would slip a pebble under Jenny Lind's saddle to make her prance about. He was also in the habit of making his sentences rhyme with a double "E," such as, "Jacob B. Moore-e is in the crowd, yea sire-e!"

As mentioned before, Moore loved to drink in large quantities. Once while visiting the home of a neighbor, the man brought out a bottle and all the time he was pouring the brandy he extolled its fine qualities, mentioning it was seven years old. After having a taste and swirling the minute remainder in the glass, Moore asked, "Did you say this is seven years old?"

"Yes," the neighbor boasted.

"Well, if that's the case," said Moore, "it's very small for its age."

WAR NEWS FROM YORK COUNTY

A few days prior to the abandonment of Lacey's Fort by the American forces, Captain David Hopkins was one of many there in bivouac. As they awaited word to move, Hopkins took the opportunity to write his sons who were living in Cumberland County, Virginia. After bringing his sons up to date on the war in South Carolina, he gave them instructions on how to save his slaves from capture.

My Dear Sons:

I find times are much worse than when you left South Carolina Last. The enemy had taken off only five of the Negroes and they on Ferguson's defeat were left to themselves and chose to come home. And on Tuesday Evening the 7th of last month Genl. Sumpter arrived at the Fish Dam Ford on Broad River & the next morning about one o'clock were attacked by the British. After contest of about an hour the enemy saw cause to quit the ground with the loss of 27 killed. We lost 5 men killed & six wounded. My boy Morris, whom I so much esteemed, I believe is mortally wounded as he is shot between the body and shoulder and bayoneted in three different places in the Body.

Capt. Charles Sims concluded to run his Negroes for Virginia. I prevailed on him to agree to try to take mine with his and told him to take them to you if possible. I also told him to be sure to tell you that if you could possibly save the Negroes from the enemy, that all should be your absolute right and property.

Capt. Sims has left the Negroes on the Yadkin River opposite the Moravian town. I would recommend you both to push immediately to where the Negroes are and run them with all speed into Virginia…save them if possible as they have been taken and retaken and if it should be the will of providence that I do survive the war I shall and do relinquish all my right[s] to all and every Negroes. All the other part of my estate except my lands had fell into the hands of the enemy. They drove off at one time between ninety and a hundred head of cattle to Winnsborough. They have also got all my sheep and the greatest part of my hogs, plantation tools, household furniture and every other article that was of any value, so that I am properly situated for a soldier and am determined to see the contest of our cause or fail in the attempt. Your Loving Father till Death.

David Hopkins

The Devil Had
Such Power

In the early years of the 1800s the people of the extreme western portion of the county lived to themselves and had little contact with law and order and often meted out a quick execution of common law. Sometime between 1835 and 1840, Morgan Martin Jr. murdered his cousin Rebecca Trull and disposed of her body in a watery grave on the Broad River. Supposedly, they were working in a cornfield when they got into a heated argument. Martin, in the heat of his anger, struck Becky in the head with a hoe. In hopes of reviving her, he knelt beside her and shook her, but to no avail. Fearing retaliation from their families, Martin carried her body to the river and buried it there in a secret grave near the mouth of Bear Creek.

The Martin family was powerful and was feared for the justice they could deliver. When Morgan's family discovered what he had done his brothers threatened to kill him. To escape from their rough judgment Morgan fled to Georgia.

Years later, in 1867, Morgan Martin wrote to his youngest brother, Thomas, from Dawson County, Georgia, to speak of his contrite heart concerning the death of Rebecca. It was a touchy situation because the Martins were not only hotheaded and unlikely to forgive and forget; the family was also powerful and few wanted to cross anyone in the family. For example, Thomas Martin married Permela Ramsey, who was called the "cowbell" of Mormonism in York County. At the time Mormons in the area were hated and could expect to be violently run out of the county. When it was learned that Permela had converted to Mormonism and was aiding and abetting Mormon missionaries, many wanted to physically chastise her as they had done others, but they knew that it would anger the Martins and ignite a feud that would be uncontrollable.

Morgan wrote to his brother:

> "I take my seat to try and write to you a few lines this morning to let you and all the rest know that I'm well. Also the rest of the family. Thanks to the heavenly blessings bestowed on us that we are together as a family and doing the best we can [with] what little time we have to live. I am thankful to God for His blessings that He has bestowed even as it is that father and mother are blessed to live to such an old age. And that so many of us are yet alive, though some are gone. I trust we will all do better for the time to come that we may all meet in heaven in

A new mobile advertisement in Clover. *Courtesy of the Museum of Western York County.*

the great day of promise of our Lord Jesus Christ. I want to see you all and be with you, if it was possible. I never would have left you in my life if it had not been that the Devil had such powers, that my peace was destroyed, and there was too many devils there. I want to live in peace."

Morgan's letter sounded as though he was truly contrite and desired peace, but Dawson County records prove differently. Six years after he wrote Thomas, he was found guilty on an assault and battery charge on Jane Bruce. Two years later his son, Michael, appeared before the Superior Court of Dawson County saying he was in fear for his life and the life of his mother, Mesina. Morgan Martin was arrested and found guilty. When the time came, he waived a trial and was placed under bond. The next year he was judged and ordered to pay all costs. It would seem that Morgan's contrite heart died and was buried and no longer seen, just like the heart of Rebecca Trull, whose body was never found.

SHE RODE AWAY ON A BAY HORSE

Ezekiel Gillham was born in 1776 and at the end of his life was buried in Bullock's Creek Presbyterian cemetery. When he was past sixty, his young wife abandoned him in 1840. Gillham notified the public by a notice in the *Yorkville Compiler*. The notice, however, appears that he was more interested in the return of his horse rather than his wife: "Whereas my wife, Elizabeth, has left my house and home and abandoned my bed and board without cause or provocation—this is to notify all persons not to harbor or entertain the said Elizabeth, or the law will be enforced against them. I will pay no debts that she may contract. She rode away on a bay horse above sixteen hands high belonging to me and also carried off a sidesaddle, my property; any person who trades for, uses, or in any manner interferes with said horse and saddle, I will hold responsible."

This notice appeared in the *Yorkville Compiler* on June 15, 1840. Just eleven days later, on June 26, Elizabeth gave birth to a son, Thomas Ezekiel Gillham. It is unknown what happened to Elizabeth, but the baby was presented to the father, who died three years later. Ezekiel's will placed the boy into the hands of his "trusty friend," twenty-one-year-old Jane Black, and made her the guardian of all his property until Thomas reached adulthood. The boy died at the age of sixteen and all Gillham property fell to Jane, who later married Matthew Bankhead. The imagination wonders and wanders over the possible answers.

THE EUDILICUS

The first 1938 reports of the African Eudilicus roaming the mill villages and streets of Rock Hill were reported in the *Evening Herald* on February 5. From its first sighting in the Arcadia mill village, it began to expand its range over other parts of town. Its descriptions were as wide and varied as its reported sightings. One said it was the size of a small calf and another said it was more the size of a gorilla and still another said it was the size of a man and made grunting sounds. Two other conflicting reports described it as being large and black and small and sleek. Whatever its shape or size, the Eudilicus had a nasty disposition. One man reported he encountered the beast between the villages of Rock Hill and Ebenezer and it tore off his clothes. Another man, while he was rushing away from the creature and looking over his shoulder, ran into a telephone pole and nearly knocked himself unconscious. Not only were the townspeople being terrorized, but many claimed the creature also delighted in taunting dogs, which returned scratched and with ears torn.

Within two days of the first report the Rock Hill police began compiling information on the Eudilicus, its sightings and activities. The *Evening Herald* offered its services as well. A reporter went to York to interview an animal trainer with the circus that winter quartered in the courthouse town. The trainer verified that none of his circus animals had escaped, and had no idea what an African Eudilicus was. During its nocturnal roamings, it was seen in Rock Hill's Cherry Park and the nearby villages of Ebenezer, Newport, Willowbrook and at the city dump. The roving terror had at least some effect on employment. The president of the Peoples National Bank reported that his maid refused to come to work, saying she would not put a foot outside her door in the early morning hours when the beast was apt to be on the streets.

The strange sightings continued on into April, when a local columnist, known for his wise and sage old advice, declared the existence of the Eudilicus was nothing more than a hoax. Robert Ward, a Rock Hill attorney who worked at the newspaper, admitted he created the original story on a particularly slow news day. He explained he had gotten the name of the fictitious beast Eudilicus from a local resident who detested Roosevelt's New Deal. The name simply meant "New Deal I cuss."

"I'll Never Come Back to York County Again!"

In 1848, during the Mexican War, John D. Quinn was stationed at Camp Meir in Mexico. Like other soldiers who are far from home, he was experiencing loneliness and wanted to hear from family and friends back home. He expressed his feelings and frustration in a letter to a friend, Joseph W. Templeton. He noted how disappointed he was in his friends not answering his letters and how his own family had let him down without a note. He wrote:

> *I take the opportunity of informing you that I am well and hoping when these lines comes to hand, [they] may find you all enjoying the same blessing. I received your letter yesterday which gave me great satisfaction to hear from you [and] to hear you were all well at that time. I would like to see you all, but God only knows when. I would like to get out of the scrape; there is some prospect of peace here, it is generally thought that [we] will be on our way home in six or eight weeks. I hope it is true, for I long to get out of this scrape once more and I will keep out of it—I am sure of it. A soldier's life is not what it is cract up to be. I am tired of it. All young men that think anything of themselves, they had better stay at home. A soldier's life is one Devil of a life to live. I never intend to show my face in Carolina again. If I was discharged now, I would not come back to Carolina. I am sure I have wrote some thirty letters to York District and I never received answers yet. Tell them that I wrote to, that I am much obliged to them for their kindness to me. I don't keer a dam whether I ever hear from them again or not. I can think as little of them as they can think of me. I am a soldier now but I hope I will not be long. See and if I live to get out of this scrape I will remember them…I am going to Texas or Mississippi. You might swear that I never will come back to York again. When*

a people is above writing to me, you are the only man that has wrote to me since I left York. My connections have treated me very bad indeed.

Tell my Mother that I am well and in hopes of getting out of this place. Tell Mr. Davidson and Mrs. Davidson that I wish them much joy and give them by best respects & tell them to write to me and let me know how a new life seems.

I have got off the notion of the girls and they pester my mind very little. The people say that bought wit is the best of wit if you do not pay too dear for it, but I have paid very dear for mine. It is very good schooling for me. I will know how to keep out of the next. Give my best respects to your father and mother and brothers and sisters. Tell them I would like to see them but only [God] knows when. I remember the pleasant hours I have spent with you all but no one knows when I ever will have the chance to be with you all again. I hope you will write to me as soon as you get this letter and let me know how you all are getting along. I want you to send me one of John E. Grist's papers and I will be much obliged to you for it.

THE FIRST FLOUR SACKS

Oral history has it that flour was first shipped in cloth sacks instead of wooden barrels from York in 1852. It was said that an unusually large crop of wheat had been harvested and barrel makers could not keep up with the demand. Needing to fill his contracts while the market value remained high, broker and farmer Thomas S. Jefferies knew he had to take desperate steps. As this supply of wheat continued to accumulate, Jefferies risked shipping in sacks. The experiment proved so successful in both handling and profit that it became the standard means of shipping by the industry.

WINDY FRIDAY

Friday, March 9, 1855, fell on the state like a day of judgment. Destructive fires driven by high winds burned over great tracts of land, burning everything in their path. Several towns were burned to the ground and some counties were completely burned over.

Across York County the wind blew like a tornado from about nine o'clock that morning until after sundown. Sometime during the morning a forest fire in Union County jumped the Broad River at Manning's plantation above King's Creek and swept over the plantation of William Whisonant, burning everything but a few panels of a rail fence. Thousands of acres above King's Creek, known as the Coaling Ground, were so burned over that hardly a house or cord of wood was left. Raging fires surged through the timberlands and skipped from hilltop to hilltop. Hopewell Independent Presbyterian Church was burned to the ground and by three in the afternoon the sun was hardly visible from the blinding and stifling smoke.

Through the state the wind unroofed houses and shook them to their foundations and fires from the fireplaces were picked up and scattered, causing hundreds of new fires. Mothers gathered up their children and what few belongings they could carry and fled to open fields while fire consumed everything they had. The shouts of men and cries of women and children were drowned out by howling winds and roaring flames. Men rode horseback for miles to help save the lives and property in western York County. As evening fell, the landscape was aglow with ten thousand fires. Eventually the winds calmed and the fires burned themselves out. For decades, those that had experienced the horrors of "Windy Friday" recalled the day each year and memorialized the day with their own personal accounts.

DARWIN'S FALSE ACCOUNTS

During the early decades of the nineteenth century, Jackey Darwin operated a store on his King's Creek farm. Darwin always kept a good supply of whiskey, since the demand equaled the supply. There were, however, some who belonged to temperance societies and openly opposed the consumption of alcoholic beverages. These teetotalers had made themselves well known throughout the area and Darwin began to find a way to have a little fun at their expense. When one of these teetotalers passed by on their way to the mill without speaking, Darwin would "charge" them with a drink or two and hang the slate outside in full view of everyone who came to do business. Not only did this make the prohibitionists appear to be hypocrites, but also their opposition to his business had little effect.

Sweet dreams at the still. *Courtesy of the Museum of Western York County.*

About the same time that Darwin was running his false black list against teetotalers, the worth of temperance societies was being debated. In August 1840, J.W. Neel, president of the Sulfur Spring Debating Society, denounced temperance leagues as a deterrent to society:

> *May God protect us from any and everything that favors aristocracy. May He guard us from any system that trammels the poor, and prohibits free trade in any article of commerce…Intemperance is an evil no one pretends to deny; and I have no doubt that everyone would put a stop to it, but not by Temperance Societies, not by legislation, but by the mighty sweep of religion and public opinion. Nothing can effect the morals of a community but the spread of religion and the happy effects of the light of the Gospel.*

Thirty-nine Lashes and a Train Ticket

Northern abolitionists began arriving in York County during the 1850s and up to the eve of the Civil War were holding secret meeting with slaves in hopes of inciting insurrection. One recorded incident illustrates the heat and excitement this provoked among the people. The episode began when a slave, Dave Burris, who was about to be punished for stealing, decided he might escape discipline by offering information on a family of abolitionists who were living in the area. He claimed that that the Tom Pugh family, who had moved into the neighborhood from Indiana, were saying there was going to be a war and when the young men would leave for the battlefields, they would gather the slaves together, rob the people of their money, take what young women they wanted and march to a free state. As Dave had planned, he escaped his punishment. When other leading men of the community were told Dave's story they became very concerned, but wondered if they should believe it since Dave was trying to avoid punishment. But then the Pughs were from one of the states that exhibited their hatred for slavery. Several days later while at a local store a woman of ill repute who consorted with the Pughs told the men that something was up at the Pugh home. It was then decided that something had to be done to get rid of the suspected abolitionists.

Knowing that the Pughs were involved in selling liquor, the men decided to build a case against them for selling to slaves and get them out of the country without bringing up the story of slave insurrection. Dave was to play a special role in their plan. On the night decided Dave and about twenty-five armed men rode to within a quarter-mile of the Pugh house and dismounted. Dave was given final instructions. He and one of the white men were to go to the house, where Dave would ask to buy a pint of whiskey; with that done the men would rush the house and take the Pughs captive.

In darkness Dave and another man crept to the house. Once there the white man took a position out of sight at the chimney corner. Dave proceeded to the door and knocked. The younger Tom Pugh came to the door and asked what the black man wanted. Whiskey. Tom asked Dave who was with him and was told he had two other slaves from a nearby plantation. Tom picked up a keg of whiskey, shook it as if he was going to pour some into a smaller container, hesitated and set down the keg. Grabbing a nearby shotgun, he threatened, "Damn you, what made you betray me?" Dave, however, seeing him reach for the gun, made a dash for the yard gate. Tom fired and filled Dave's backside with shot. When Tom jumped out the door he saw a man step out of the shadows. He opened fire with a "pepper box" pistol and peppered the chimney near the man. Tom's fire was returned by the man, who had a Navy Colt six-shooter and was no better shot than Tom: he emptied all six shots at Pugh, who was not more than ten feet away. Only the sixth burned a path across the bootlegger's belly.

At the sound of the firing, the rest of the men came at a dead run. Pugh popped back into the house and slammed the door after the exchange of fire. The men stormed the house, broke down the door and surrounded the Pughs, who momentarily surrendered. One man swung his Colt to shoot the elder Tom Pugh, but another man hit his man just as he fired and the bullet just parted the old man's hair. The younger man cried out, "Men, if you want to kill me take me out of sight of my family, don't kill me before their eyes."

The house and grounds were given a thorough search. In the corncrib they found a boy of about seven years old, chained like a dog, with only an old quilt for a bed. He was not a Pugh, but an orphan. He was released and later placed in the custody of a local man and apprenticed or "bound out" until he came of age. The next day a public hearing was held, at which time it was decided that all the property of the Pughs would be sold at a public auction and paid in gold. The magistrate also ordered the two men to receive thirty-nine lashes on bare backs. This was quickly administered by an overseer from a nearby plantation.

Train tickets were purchased for the family and when they were placed on the train a placard was put on both Toms: "Abolitionist—Pass them on boys." It was told that when they got back to Indiana, young Tom enlisted in the Northern army.

How to Break a Husband of Drinking

Shortly after Luke Smith and Nancy Walker were married, oats ripened and the harvest began. Early in the morning Young Luke would be busy in his fields with his scythe and cradle. As it happened the regular mustering of the militia took place and, after cutting oats in the morning, Luke went off to

Taking a break at a moonshine still. *Courtesy of the Museum of Western York County.*

perform his patriotic duty. Whiskey flowed heavily at these musters and on this particular day, Luke took too much of the jug and when he struck out for home, he was stepping mighty high. Nancy saw her groom coming down the road, three sheets to the wind. Suppressing her disgust she met him with her happiest mood. When he went out to the field to bundle the oats, he could hardly stand and every time he bent over he would pitch forward and nearly fall on his face. When Nancy saw the pitiful condition her husband was in, she went out and told him she would bundle and tie the oats. He protested, but she said ever so sweetly, "Oh, no honey, you're in no fix to work now; I'll tie them up for you."

Luke later claimed that was the first and only time Nancy ever saw him drunk and her sweetness caused him to swear off liquor from that day forward.

Years later, after Nancy died, Luke had some interest in remarrying and he made this known among the men and women of the area. Hardly a single woman passed about whom he did not make a remark. Some claimed he was not really interested in marriage but that it was his way of hiding his sorrow in the loss of his wife, as well as two sons in the Civil War.

On one occasion he made a comment comparing one widow with another, saying Mrs. Beard was a lady beside Mrs. Hamrick. When Mrs. Hamrick heard what he had said, she resolved to confront him and ask for an explanation. It was not long before they met and she asked, "Mr. Smith, what remark was that you made about me the other day?"

"I don't know except I said you were good looking or something like that," he replied.

"No, it was not that," she pressed. "You said that Mrs. Beard was a lady by the side of me, and I want you to explain yourself."

"Well, I can do that mighty quick," he said. "I said it and I meant it. I said she was a lady by the side of you, and I meant that you were a lady by the side of her, when you were both together. I meant that both of you were ladies." Thus he turned a rude remark to his advantage.

JOSEPH KERR:
REVOLUTIONARY WAR SPY

On October 4, 1780, British Colonel Patrick Ferguson camped at Cowpens planning to rendezvous with General Cornwallis at Charlotte. Little did he know that over the mountain, Patriots from Tennessee were camped only twenty miles away and that Colonel Edward Lacey and his troops were moving in his direction. The next day Ferguson and his command crossed the Broad River at Adair's Ferry and bivouacked about a mile from the ferry on the plantation of Peter Quinn. That evening Joseph Kerr, a Patriot spy, strolled into Ferguson's camp.

Crippled from infancy, he was unable to serve in the militia but had been offered work as a secret agent for General McDowell. His first task was to investigate the movements of the Tories on Tyger River and infiltrate their camp. He barely escaped with his life when he posed as a Tory and entered the camp of Christian Huck, where he was identified as a "damn rebel spy." Holding a sword over Kerr's head with threatening gestures, Huck demanded the truth, but the young man denied any association with the American Patriots. The captain warned Kerr, "Young man, I am damn suspicious of you. You could do us more harm than two hundred fighting men in the field." Huck promised to spare his life if he would remain in the camp and take an oath of allegiance to the king. Kerr agreed, but at his first opportunity he escaped to Captain Barnett. After Barnett debriefed Kerr, the captain began making plans to attack Huck with only thirty-one men. Fortunately, others joined Barnett's men, resulting in the Battle of Williamson's Plantation and the death of Captain Huck.

At Ferguson's camp on the banks of the Broad River, Kerr learned the colonel was planning to mount the summit of King's Mountain and wait for reinforcements from Charlotte. In the night Kerr slipped out of the camp and headed back to Cowpens to inform Colonel Lacey. The next day, Ferguson pushed northward, crossed King's Creek and made camp atop the mountain. The area was heavily populated with Loyalists and as soon as Ferguson arrived, he immediately sent out men to enlist their services. Emboldened, the would-be recruiters instead took up plundering the homes of Patriots.

When Kerr reached the Patriots at Cowpens, the leaders immediately called a council to plan their encounter with Ferguson. Nine hundred and ten men made a night march to the mountain. Later Colonel Hill would call this regiment "a flying column." The rest of the story is well known. Few, however, know that the reconnaissance of a small, handicapped Patriot played a major role in bringing about a devastating defeat of the British known as the turning point of the American Revolution in the South.

A PENSION FOR OLD PHILLIP

Twenty-three-year-old John Roseboro left his widowed mother, Ellen, in charge of their Turkey Creek plantation while he answered his country's call. Along with John went his body servant, Phillip, who was charged with taking care of the young man. John Roseboro won rapid promotion and soon received a captain's commission. This promotion also brought Phillip into close contact with other officers, who immediately took a liking to the body servant. While repulsing an attack at Seven Pines a shell killed John and Phillip received a leg wound. Despite his wounds, Phillip and a soldier carried John's body back to his South Carolina home.

Shortly after the funeral, "Missus Ellen" called Phillip to the "big house" and charged him to return to the battlefields with her son-in-law, Captain James Williamson, and watch over him just as he had done John. "Cap'n Jim" was killed at Drewry's Bluff. Phillip remained among the officers who had befriended him and was later captured along with a number of soldiers. From April to July he was held a prisoner, but Phillip recalled, "Dem Yankees had no use fer [me] and dey turned me loose."

In total Phillip served four years in the Confederate army and in spite of the hardships he later recalled his fondest memories were seeing Grant and Lee at Appomattox and making coffee for General Jackson. It took Phillip three weeks to walk from the Virginia battlefields to the Roseboro plantation. He expected to find everything as he had left it, but the world had been turned upside down: Many of the freedmen had taken flight and only his former mistress and daughter were left. In the years that followed, Phillip and his family stayed on the plantation and did all they could to eke out a living until death claimed the Roseboros and Phillip's wife. Their eleven children grew up and scattered themselves abroad. Lame and bending over from age and years of labor, Phillip was cast into the world, where he wandered for a while, finally settling near Shelby, North Carolina.

Regardless of his age, farmers and lumbermen of the area recognized Phillip Roseboro as one of the best woodcutters in the county. As late as 1925, he was still able to produce two cords of wood in a day. Nearly everyone—both black and white—knew and appreciated the old man. Often he was seen trudging up Shelby Street toward the post office with an axe on his shoulder, dragging along one foot and bringing up the other with a jerk. His face was wrinkled and his head was topped with white hair. He was a pitiful but well-honored sight in his tattered clothing and coonskin hat as he made his way to pick up his pension for "fighting the Yankees along with Capt'ns John and Jim."

Hickory Grove High School baseball team, circa 1912. *Courtesy of the Museum of Western York County.*

TIED-UP AND DID

Around 1860 there lived a couple near Hickory Grove who were real characters: "Tied-up" and her husband, "Did," Sandlin. We are not sure how Did got his nickname, but Margaret Laney Sandlin, sometimes called Peggy, earned hers from her habit of tying up her husband every time he got drunk—which was quite often. She gained a reputation among the superstitious as a fortuneteller with supernatural powers. James L. Strain wrote:

> For her, the superstitious had the highest respect and would turn the cup or cut the cards according to her orthodox rules, while under an assumed power of divination she would proceed to unfold the decree of an unknown future to her fortunate victims. She had gained a reputation almost as notorious of that of the Witch of Endor…cows were made to climb the sides of houses; coffee pots and kettles made to boil over an insignificant amount of coals; milk cows made to go dry or give milk…with her died the last vestige of antique heresy in western York County.

On one occasion Did and Tied-up went to the Henry Whisonant farm to see a calf that was reported to have been bitten by a mad dog and was insane. A number of others came by to see the curiosity. Before Did and Tied-up arrived at the farm the Whisonant children and their friends had been teasing the calf and got it in the habit of running after its tormentors. However, when the Sandlins and John Childers arrived the calf was lying down and taking no notice of anyone or anything. Did concluded it was dead and got into the pen and roughly nudged it with his foot and the calf rolled to one side. Tied-up suggested, "Twist its tail, Did, that'll move it, if it ain't dead." Did grabbed up its tail and gave a mighty twist and the calf sprung to its feet. The calf made a lunge toward Did and the old man made a break for the fence, which had been built higher than usual to retain the mad calf. To make matters worse, Did had to run uphill. John Childers shouted, "Look out, Did, here it comes!" Did made a dive for the top rail of the fence but miscalculated and yanked the rail off on him, doing him more damage than the calf. Some time later Whitaker "Whit" Ramsey went to see the oddity and had the same experience as Did. Both men were the objects of derision for a long time, giving men and women hearty laughs.

York County's First Ground Hog

The 1850 federal census reveals that Robert Whitesides and his family must have lived comfortably in western York County, with fifteen slaves and real estate valued at $13,000. Although Whitesides was one of the wealthiest men in that part of the county, his sons were used to putting in a full day of hard labor. As one of the wealthier plantation owners, Whitesides easily could afford to be a progressive farmer with his eye on modern machinery.

Around 1850, he purchased York County's first field thresher, sometimes called a "Ground Hog." While these were a great improvement over threshing grain by hand and supposed to be a laborsaving machine, it took seven men and six mules to operate the contraption. The "Ground Hog" was a good investment since Whitesides could contract with surrounding farmers to bring the machine to their fields and thresh their oats, wheat and rye for a price. Whitesides took full advantage of this and in 1852 contracted with nearly every farmer in the area and threshed nearly six thousand bushels that season.

The first reported fatal accident caused by the thresher took place two years later when a spike from the machine struck James Bryant in the eye and killed him instantly. That accident took place on a plantation owned by a kinsman of Robert Whitesides.

Stargazing at Unity Cemetery

Elisha Atkins was one of the more outstanding characters of antebellum western York County who lived in the vicinity of Hickory Grove. He was described as being crude and unpolished, "cunning as a fox, vindictive as an adder, and revengeful as an Indian." He had an excellent memory—property lines, landmarks and the roots of old arguments and feuds were his specialty. He could monopolize the conversation and talk all night without telling his listener the same thing twice. His greatest vice was profanity and he seldom went to church, but knew the Bible well enough to argue either side of a doctrine.

Atkins was a widower who fancied himself an eligible bachelor. In 1857 some European astronomer predicted that a comet would strike and destroy the earth on June 18; many grew fearful as the day approached. As it happened, the day it was to appear was the same day that Gainey Bolin was to be buried at Unity Church. Before the body was brought to the cemetery, the gravediggers were joined by a number of people who came for the funeral; among these were "Lige" Atkins and a number of young women the old man imagined were prospects for a wife.

It was about two o'clock in the afternoon as the people began to assemble and they were all abuzz about the prediction of the comet. At that hour Venus was high overhead and in close conjunction with the sun, which caused the crowd to peer into the heavens. "Lige" Atkins had lost all of his front teeth and because of his snags was nicknamed "Forks." Looking upward toward the sun, Atkins could not help but wince and grimace, showing his gaps and snags. The sight created laughter from some of the young women and the old man mistook their giggles for admiration. When he found out they were having fun at his expense he exploded with profanity and told them he had more sense than them or their mamas.

How High, Daddy?

When William Strain moved into York County from Fairfield he settled on Guyon Moore Creek just north of Smith's Ford. There he built a log cabin and raised his family. As log houses were prone to do, one of the walls settled on one side, causing a rafter to rest on a cupboard, making it nearly impossible to open the doors. One of his sons figured they needed to lift part of the wall until the rafter cleared the cupboard and place a wedge between the logs to keep that section from dropping back down. Preparations were made to do the work and a pivot and prying pole was readied to lift the wall. The young man left the old man and his helpers outside to pry up the wall while he called back when the rafter cleared the cupboard. The old man, however, did not quite understand the process and instead of placing the prying pole between the floor and the wall, he put it under the sill. Inside, young Strain knew something was not going right when the entire end of

Young members of Yorkville Masonic Order, circa 1890. *Courtesy of the Museum of Western York County*.

the cabin was moving upward. Realizing the pry pole had been put under the sill he knew that even if the entire end of the cabin was lifted off its foundation it would never free the cupboard. He called out in fun, "Daddy, what are you doing?"

The old man replied, "I'm prying the house off the cupboard!"

"Well Daddy," the son shouted in return, "just how high do you think you will have to go?"

LACEY'S FORT

Lacey's Revolutionary War fort, sometimes called "Liberty Hill," was built to hinder the British in their push into the Backcountry as well as offer protection for area families. Colonel Edward Lacey selected the site, which was on a hilltop on Turkey Creek, about five miles east of the Bullock's Creek meeting house. Here, on the road from Charleston and Camden to the North Carolina forts, a blockhouse with an earthen redoubt was built. From here the American Patriots would monitor the main road as well as the nearby Hamilton's and Love's Fords on the Broad River. The British sometimes referred to Lacey's Fort as "Rebel's Folly," but one historian said it was far from a folly, since not one British unit was able to get past the redoubt.

Following the defeat of the British at King's Mountain on October 7, 1780, Lacey and his men retired to the fort for rest and to await further orders. Near the end of October General Sumter arrived and took command. The general led the Patriots across the Broad to harass the British stockades in that area. In their movements Sumter and his men met with Georgia troops under the command of Colonels John Twiggs, Andrew Pickens and Elijah Clarke. In a strategy meeting it was agreed that both forces would march against the Tories located at Ninety Six, on the British's most formidable stronghold. Lacey and his men remained at the Turkey Creek fort well into December, still active in recruiting troops from York and Chester Counties. Toward the end of December the American forces were making plans to evacuate the fort. Elsewhere, about December 25, General Green divided his troops. Colonel William Washington's light infantry and cavalry were reassigned to General Daniel Morgan. They were ordered to advance to Ninety Six, passing between the Catawba and Broad Rivers to collect the militia in those districts. Upon reading General Green's orders Lacey and his men broke camp and marched their regiment under General Morgan until after the Battle of Cowpens.

Ghostly Secrets, Daredevil Preachers and Walking on Water

A few days later, Cornwallis heard of Lacey abandoning the fort and the British lord began preparing for a trek into North Carolina. He sent Ban Tarleton ahead with instructions to cross to the west side of the Broad River to force Morgan northward. On January 7 Cornwallis sent a message to Tarleton telling him where he would be. They reached the crossroads near the Bullock's Creek Church the following Saturday. All along the way, Cornwallis's Tories practiced their art of plundering and horse stealing. By the time they arrived at the fort on Turkey Creek they had amassed a large number of horses.

The roads were dreadful throughout their march. Cornwallis camped for some time at Bull Run in Chester County waiting for General Leslie's command to join them, but Leslie was delayed by high waters and would not clear the swamps until January 14. When Leslie delayed, Cornwallis could wait no longer and wrote Tarleton of his delay and when he expected to arrive at the Hillhouse plantation near the fort. On the fourteenth when Lord Cornwallis penned his message to Tarleton, he had already crossed the Broad River near the mouth of Turkey Creek. He was destined to clash with Morgan two days later at Cowpens.

As Cornwallis planned, he arrived at the William Hillhouse plantation and Lacey's Fort on January 16. The following morning, at eight o'clock, Tarleton came within sight of General Morgan's camp at a place known as "the Cowpens." Expecting to find the Americans in retreat, to his surprise they were arrayed for battle. The history of the American Revolution contains no more wonderful battle than that of Cowpens. The advantages were all on the side of the British, yet the Americans won the day. The American loss was 12 killed and 58 wounded. By their own account, the British loss numbered 100 killed with 523 taken prisoner; 35 wagons of baggage fell into the hands of the Americans along with 800 horses, 2 artillery pieces and 800 muskets. As Tarleton fled the battlefield he received Cornwallis's message of being delayed by Leslie. The colonel was furious to learn that the general was not in the prearranged position on the west side of the Broad River. Joined by approximately 200 of his fleeing cavalry and fugitives, Tarleton turned eastward and crossed the river at Hamilton's Ford. Others had fled farther southward to Love's Ford.

On the morning of January 18 Major General Alexander Leslie marched into the Cornwallis camp; with him came a force of 1,350 men. Within hours, Tarleton arrived and delivered the news of his defeat. Tradition relates that General Cornwallis was leaning on his sword when receiving the news of Tarleton's defeat and he became so furious that his sword snapped under his weight. Whether this happened or not, it was told and seen as an omen of the coming surrender of the British.

Lord Cornwallis prepared to move toward North Carolina. Tarleton and his remaining troops were ordered to recross the Broad River at Hamilton's Ford and try to unite with soldiers still scattered from the battle. At eight o'clock on the morning of January 19, Cornwallis gave the order to move forward. Jaegers, or mounted infantrymen with rifles, led the column and were followed by a corps of road cutters or "pioneers." In order to pass up the trail, the British pioneers cleared and widened the road; for that reason the road would later be known as the "King's Road." The remaining column consisted of two three-pound cannons followed by a brigade of guards, the Von Bose Regiment and then by the North Carolina Tories. Protecting the army's rear were two six-pound cannons, followed by Lieutenant Colonel Webster's cavalry brigade. Wagons carrying the baggage of the field officers and the clothing and furniture of General Cornwallis followed. Finally came the ammunition wagons, hospital and regimental wagons, the provision train and loose horses. One hundred men selected from Colonel Webster's brigade formed the rear of the column.

Behind the caravan was total devastation; everything had been destroyed. On the morning of their departure the British burned the plantation of Isaac Haney located just south of the camp in what is now Chester County. A great mass of land on the Hillhouse plantation had also been completely deforested. In June 1832 William Hillhouse wrote to the War Department describing the appearance of his plantation after quartering the British troops for four days: "I would also state to the War Department that the British Commander-in-Chief, Lord Cornwallis on his march to Virginia in January 1781 made my plantation his place of rendezvous from Tuesday till Thursday, stripped me of all my possessions except the land which he could not destroy."

A BETTER PREACHER THAN A TRADER

Reverend Madison Mullinax pastored Unity Baptist Church in Hickory Grove sometime during the mid-1800s. Two of the church's more outstanding members during his pastorate were Joe and Polly Leech. "Governor," as Joe was called, was an uneducated man, but it was said there was no better trader in livestock anywhere in the county, and that he could instantly tell the value of a horse by looking at its eyelashes and the sides of its neck.

Leech's wife, "Miss Polly," was a kind and generous woman who took pity on her preacher, who was so poor he could not afford a milk cow. One day she told Joe that she wanted to give Mr. Mullinax a cow and that he should bring the preacher over and let him chose a good milk cow. At first the preacher refused, but Joe insisted and brought him over to his cow lot. After the preacher made his choice, Leech told him that he had picked out a very good cow, but certainly not the best in the lot. Leech showed him another cow and went into some details explaining the good qualities, saying this was the one he should have. When the preacher agreed he would take the better cow, Leech then told him that if he would give him eight dollars to boot, he would gladly swap cows. The preacher accepted the offer, believing he had made a good deal.

"I Want to Swing Heavy Today"

In the county courthouse the voice of Judge O'Neal rang solemnly:

> *James Vickers, Newton Vickers: young men. The conviction, to which your attention has just been called, makes you aware of your awful impending doom. The 27th day of July last, is a day red with blood—a day on which the blood of your fellow man cried unto God from the ground. Its voice has been heard and will be answered beyond the grave. Young men, I learn from your trial that you are orphans; that you have been brought up in gross ignorance; then let me, in the discharge of a most solemn and painful duty, point you to the Lamb of God which taketh away the sin of the world. Let me urge upon you to pray, pray night and day. Pray earnestly, and if you can't so much as lift up voices in prayer, do like the Publican of old, smite upon your breasts and cry, "God be merciful to me a sinner."*

For the murder of William Dobson in a Rock Hill barroom, James and Newton Vickers were sentenced to be hanged on December 29, 1854. Samuel Youngblood, the sheriff of York County, was required by law to be the executioner. Being kind-hearted and good-natured, the sheriff was loath to perform this part of his duty, yet he was cognizant that he could not avoid it. In an idle conversation Sheriff Youngblood said he would give twenty-five dollars to any man who would hang

York County Courthouse, Yorkville, South Carolina, circa 1850. *Courtesy of the Museum of Western York County.*

the Vickers boys. Standing nearby was John McGowan, who was nicknamed "By Granny McGowan." McGowan stepped up and said, "By granny, I'll hang them for it!"

By the time the sun rose over Yorkville on the day of execution, Newton Vickers had received a pardon from the governor. The brothers were confined to the same cell until death would separate them. Sheriff Youngblood came into the cell and, after speaking with them, asked what they wanted for breakfast. Newton had no stomach for food, but James replied, "Bring me a good breakfast; I want to swing heavy today." The streets of Yorkville were filled with horses, wagons, buggies and pedestrians. Colonel Sadler formed his militia guards and marched them to the old jail. A great crowd followed. The guards formed a semicircle at the entrance and allowed a wagon to back up to the door. Momentarily the jail door swung open and James Vickers stepped out and firmly stepped into the wagon and took a seat in the left front corner. The sheriff, his deputies and a minister followed the condemned man and took their seats. As soon as they sat down, Colonel Sadler gave the command for the unit to move forward. Leading the procession with his saber swinging left and right, he opened up a path through the teeming crowd that stretched out as far as the eye could see. The mud in many places was ankle deep, but the guards kept their pace and trudged through, finally arriving at the gallows. The wagon was driven under the beam and came to a stop.

The minister rose and made a few remarks and announced the singing of the hymn "When I Can Read My Title Clear." Peyton B. Darwin sang the hymn to the tune of "Liverpool" and was accompanied by many in the crowd who knew the hymn. The minister and the prisoner knelt as the clergyman prayed aloud. The guards and most of the men in the crowd stood quietly with their hats in hand.

When the prayer ended, the trapdoor was adjusted for the final drop. Vickers rose and removed his coat, disclosing a snow-white shroud. The good-looking young man made firm steps to the end of the wagon and stepped onto the trapdoor. He said nothing as the rope was threaded through a hole in the beam, tied and fastened to a pin in the upright post to his left, leaving about three feet of slack. His hands and feet were bound and a hood was pulled over his face. The sheriff descended the steps and took up a hatchet. The sheriff took a swing at the rope and missed and with a second, cleanly severed the rope, sending James Vickers into eternity.

LIFTING THE SKULL

Dr. J. Rufus Bratton of Yorkville requires no introduction to the readers of York County history. For many years before the Civil War, and long afterward, his services were in constant demand. At the outbreak of the Civil War he was appointed assistant surgeon of the Fifth South Carolina Regiment of Volunteers and served his first year in Georgia at the Winder Hospital. In 1862 he was put in charge of the Fourth Regiment.

Several years before the war, about 1856 or 1857, during a battalion muster at Carroll's old field near the Sharon Associate Reformed Presbyterian Church, a mare kicked in John Ramsey's skull. For many days, or perhaps weeks, while John lay suffering his family despaired over his life. Dr. Bratton was called and recommended trephining the skull to relieve the brain of pressure. When this was done (without anesthesia) Ramsey soon recovered and lived many years and enjoyed a long life with a healthy mind and body.

Another operation of this kind took place about 1890, when Dr. Joseph Saye of Sharon was stopped on the side of the road to attend to a man with a serious head wound he had received in a fight. Dr. Saye told the man that his skull needed to be lifted off the brain to relieve the pain, but he did not have the proper instruments with him. Saye told his black patient to lean over and stay as still as possible. Saye later said,

> *Then I started lifting that broken skull. The Negro never groaned, although I know the pain was intense. Finally I paused in my operation for a moment when he raised his head and asked, "Doctor, would you mind if I smoked a cigarette?" I told him to go to it, and do you know, he calmly smoked while I cleared the brain of the cracked skull? And that Negro lived to make many a bale of cotton.*

WHEN YOU BUILD
A PIGPEN

In June of 1858, John Abel of Newton, North Carolina, was arrested in York, charged with stealing a saddle from John B. McConnell of McConnellsville.

At the time of the arrest, the saddle was in Abel's possession and on a small black mule that Abel could not account for. After Sheriff Stillwell secured Abel in the jail, he discovered the man's true name was John Jonas and that the mule belonged to Hugh McConnell of Chester.

While confined to his jail cell, the saddle thief became acquainted with a slave in an adjoining cell. For some reason, perhaps to secure his own escape, Jonas forged papers for the slave with a promise to help him escape from jail and bondage. The outcome of this plan remains uncertain, but Jonas made his escape by cutting through the plaster ceiling with a knife smuggled in to him. He broke off the lathing, passed through the opening and lowered himself to the ground using blankets tied together. John Jonas must have been something of a jokester since he left a humorous, though poorly spelled note:

> *Gentlemen: When you put a hog up to fatten always put a bottom in your pen for fear yore hog might root out. Never build your pen out of corn stalks or else your hog will gnaw them in two and when you put a man in Jail never build your Jail out of clapboards and bird trip sticks. If you want to know where I am just come down to York shire there you will find me picking chinquapins to pay tax and a lawyer to plead for all the cracks. And when the lawyers find a flaw then the Judge like any Jack will lay down what is law. This place York is mighty fine place for they will skin a flee for the hide and tallow. I want you to answer my letter if you pleas, direct your letter to Lincoln tink tank where the frogs jump from bank to bank. I doant speak of eny place, but his one horse town. You can't get this fox eny more, you can't drive him under your trap then put it down on him. You must bait with gold next time. Bait it thick as ten bumble bee in a pumpkin bloom.*

THE HORRIFIC STORM
OF 1859

At nine o'clock in the evening of May 20, 1859, black, threatening clouds began gathering over King's Mountain and moved rapidly southward. As the storm clouds gathered and widened out for a mile and a half, wind, rain, hail and lightning unleashed their full fury onto western York County. Quickly the storm stretched to a width of three or four miles and the roar of its coming destruction was described as "a thousand wagons and teams running away in a crowd." Lightning was constant, "and the whole heavens appeared to be an intensely burning sheet of flame."

Destruction resulting from the storm stretched from Clarks Fork to Hickory Grove, Hopewell, Blairsville, just east of the Bullock's Creek Church and into Chester County. Within thirty minutes the land that had been bursting with spring's shades of green resembled a winter landscape. A solid sheet of water and hail covered the area. Small branches were suddenly turned into rivers and the land was washed into gullies. Rail fences floated away, scattering the timbers for hundreds of yards over the fields and forest. Scarcely a panel of fencing was left. The hail stripped foliage from entire forests and cedars were as bare as any deciduous tree. Pines were so deprived of their needles and bark they looked as if they had been swept clean with fire. Wheat was beaten into stubble and the straw was pounded into the soil. Corn and cotton suffered the same fate. Debris was piled as high as a two-story house in the bottoms and along creeks.

The next day the land looked like the dead of winter. Hailstones the size of quail eggs drifted to the depths of two to four feet. One man told that while riding his horse that was sixteen hands high, he could easily pick up a handful without dismounting. Along Bullock's Creek hail piled up as high as fifteen feet. Three weeks after the storm Dr. Bond E. Feemster, James Guy and Dr. William McNeel reported finding hail still lying on the ground.

The hurricane-like winds lifted and carried away the roofs of houses, outhouses, barns, stables and tenant dwellings. Deprived of their roofs, many corncribs had their contents scattered for hundreds of yards. One farmer claimed that his wagon, braked and attached to a crib, was driven by the winds for fifty yards before smashing into a building. Both wagon and building were torn into hundreds of fragments. Another person reported that a rock more than three feet square was moved sixty feet. A wash pot, picked up at a spring, was tossed into a field four hundred yards away, breaking it into large fragments.

Following the storm many area farmers were faced with rebuilding and clearing the land as though they were new settlers. Houses, barns, fences, corncribs and various outbuildings had to be rebuilt. Crops had to be replanted with little hope of making a crop. Thirty minutes of destruction took years of hard work to restore the land, forests and farms.

The only death reported came from a home near the Chester and York County line. There a large log house was blown down upon its six inhabitants and an old lady, Mrs. Nelly Alberson, was instantly killed. A younger Mrs. Alberson and her six children escaped serious injury; however, her mother, Mrs. Sarah Henderson, suffered a broken leg and a fatal fractured skull.

There was no way of estimating the damage this storm wreaked upon that section of York County. It took years for farmers to recover their loss. Since the Civil War began within two years and men were called from their homes, it is likely much of the work was never accomplished. Decades would pass before a storm of this proportion was reported; only Hugo, which struck the eastern portion of the county in 1989, is comparable.

THE COUNCIL OF FLIGHT

A few years before the American Revolution, James Jamieson of Brandywine Creek, Pennsylvania, moved with his family to what is now southwest York County. In 1777 he enlisted as a private in the militia to aid in putting down a Creek Indian revolt in Georgia that was affecting the safety of Carolinians. The Georgia Expedition developed Jamieson into a seasoned soldier and paved the way for his commission to lieutenant shortly after the fall of Charleston in May 1780.

When the South Carolina capital fell to the British, the state went into shock and turmoil. In late May or early June, Colonels William Bratton and Samuel Watson assembled the New Acquisition Regiment at the Bullock's Creek meetinghouse to consider their predicament and ask the question, should they continue or surrender? Newly commissioned Lieutenant Jamieson was in attendance. After some discussion, the colonels announced that it was futile to make any further resistance to the British, and advised it was every man for himself. Jamieson was incensed over the decision, saying they were not a council of war but rather a council of flight. In frustration, Jamieson contended that there were Patriots in North Carolina who were still willing to fight for liberty and invited those who would to join with him at sunrise to begin a northward trek to find Colonel Thomas Sumter and his men. When the warm spring sun rose over the grounds of the log meetinghouse the next morning eleven men mounted their horses and rode away.

Soon word of the "council of flight" reached the ears of British Colonel Lord Rawdon in Camden. He immediately sent a commissioner to meet with people living between the Catawba and Broad Rivers. The arrival of Rawdon's representative at Hill's Iron Works was announced and area settlers began to congregate at the ironworks. The commissioner announced, "He was empowered

Hugh Sherer and Jimmy Sharp on York Street, Sharon. *Courtesy of the Museum of Western York County.*

by Lord Rawdon to receive their submissions & give paroles and protection to all who choose to become British subjects." The commissioner claimed the Continental Congress had abandoned the Carolinas and they could no longer expect support of the Continental Army. William Hill, owner of the ironworks, was inflamed by Rawdon's announcements and called them a pack of "damn lies." Hill's accusation seemed to renew the patriotic spirit in these backwoodsmen and in unison they drove the British commissioner away. They reformed militias under the command of Colonels Andrew Neel and William Hill. Like Lieutenant Jamieson they marched to North Carolina, planning to unite their forces with Sumter.

Jamieson joined with Sumter and soon received a captain's commission. At the victorious battle at Rocky Mountain Jamieson was severely wounded and was promptly sent to Charlotte to recuperate. As soon as he was able, he was sent home to complete his convalescence. Within a short time he was taken captive by a band of Tories and was taken to General Cornwallis for interrogation. During the interrogation, the general wanted to know if he had ever killed one of the king's men. Jamieson responded, "If ever I killed any of the king's men, it was in battle in defense of my country—except on one occasion [when] I killed an Indian. I know that I killed that king's man because we were alone in a personal conflict."

Jamieson was retained as a prisoner of war for a month and then released. Finally he arrived at home to recover from his wounds and the ill treatment he had received at the hands of the Tories. Jamieson was determined to return to his command, but the war ended before he was strong enough to resume his duties. He lived in peace for the rest of his life (except for a brief interlude during the War of 1812). He died at the age of eighty-one and is buried in the Bullock's Creek Presbyterian Cemetery. His tombstone proudly reads, "A Soldier and Officer of the Revolution."

HE HAD THE STOMACH OF A HANDSAW

Ben Bolin, a man who might be described as eccentric, lived in a section of western York County known as "The Nations." Ben was tall and slightly stoop-shouldered with black hair and black eyes. Though he was uneducated, he had a good deal of common sense about him, but he often acted as though he had no sense at all. He hated a hypocrite, had little appreciation for religion, as did most of his family, but he was truthful and honest. His favorite occupations were hunting and fishing. He was none too keen on working, but sometimes made shingles or did small jobs.

Ben had some peculiar habits that caused Jim Hill to say that he had the stomach of a handsaw and would do things that would gag the average person. It was nothing to see him swallow live minnows whole, and he was noted for biting the heads off black snakes.

As it happened, a black man by the name of George operated McGill's gristmill, and this man had a dog that feared nothing and would jump on any other dog that came by and make it run away in pain and humiliation. One morning after a drinking bout with Robert Manning, Ben staggered home by the way of McGill's mill. Not too inebriated to devise one of his stunts, Ben decided he was going to give George's dog the fight of his life. When he got to the mill he got down on all fours and crept up on George's dog and began to growl. Confused by the situation, George's dog tried to walk away, but Ben continued after him. Still, the dog would have nothing to do with the strange man and tried to walk away. Without warning Ben jumped on the dog and latched onto its ear and began to shake him bulldog style. Momentarily the dog was stunned, but soon his patience wore thin and he rose up to properly defend himself. Ben wrapped his arms around the dog, threw him on the ground and held him so tightly the dog could not move and finally gave up the fight. Ben pronounced himself the top dog.

When the Civil War heated up, Ben Bolin joined the Seventeenth Regiment under Captain L.P. Sadler in 1861 and was sent to Camp Hampton near Columbia for training. At these camps, young Citadel cadets were assigned as drill instructors to change farmers into soldiers. As mentioned before, Ben was stoop-shouldered and could not properly attain the posture of a soldier. As a little cadet frisked around in his spike-tail coat and gave Ben commands to straighten up, Ben's patience wore out and he said, "How do you expect to straighten a crooked man unless you put his head on the back of his neck?" He then proceeded to tell the cadet he would slap him around if he said any more about it.

OLD BILLY HARDWICK

It may have been around Christmas of 1862, as the Civil War was raging in Virginia, when seventy-year-old William Hardwick climbed out of his bed and began making preparations for a long, arduous trip. The hardship of the journey

First mail carriers in Sharon, circa 1910. *Courtesy of the Museum of Western York County.*

was not what occupied the old man's mind, but rather the anticipation of seeing his sons and giving them a few meager supplies. After eating breakfast and biding his wife and family adieu, he tied two heavy bags to his horse's back, settled himself in his saddle and set out to Virginia.

Hardwick's love for his sons, Star and Hazel, compelled him to make the journey to the battlefields of Virginia. In spite of the pleadings of his wife, "Aunt Millie," and his daughters and daughters-in-laws, he headed northward. His wit and determination served him well and he eventually arrived in Virginia and found his boys. From the two bulging bags Uncle Billy pulled out and distributed much needed socks, other articles of warm clothing and hickory nuts he had gathered near his home.

The old man shared the news from back home. The boys had a new niece born in October—Leticia, the daughter of their sister Ann and her husband, Samuel Blair. Tom Dowdle and his wife, as well as Joe Feemster and his wife, were expecting babies in January. But all was not good news. Two young Confederates had died: Amzi Clark from some disease and Sam Gill in a Charleston hospital, perhaps from wounds.

The visit was all too short; as they said their goodbyes, little did the young men know this would be the last time they would see their father. On his return trip, Uncle Billy contracted smallpox. As he neared his home in southwest York County, he knew he was getting sick, but he had no way of knowing the fatal fever would spread to his family. At home, when it was obvious he had smallpox, he was isolated in the smokehouse. "Old Sam," a faithful servant, tended to the old man until he died, which occurred within a few days. Shortly thereafter his four-month-old granddaughter, little Lettie, broke out with pox and she too died within a few days.

Mildred Hardwick struggled through the loss of her husband and granddaughter, but before the war was over, she would suffer the loss of her sons, Star and Hazel. Ann and Samuel moved in with her mother to be a comfort in her remaining days. On Christmas Day in 1879, she walked out to the smokehouse where her husband had died sixteen years earlier. Inside she had laid away some fruits and nuts for the grandchildren. As she leaned over the barrel, grappling for a choice apple, she suffered a stroke and fell to the earthen floor. She was carried back into the house, where she soon expired.

SHE AND THE NEGROES ARE ABOUT TO GET NAKED!

As the Civil War continued into its third year, many Southern troops were suffering from lack of food and clothing. Letters written home from the battlefields of Virginia were virtual want lists that begged for the most insignificant items. In January 1864, Joseph Templeton of York County, whose company was camped near Orange Courthouse, Virginia, wrote his sister: "I want you to send me some cowpeas. I never was so starved in all my life. And I want a pone of bread and some potatoes if you have them to spare."

Those civilians whose doorsteps faced the battlefields joined the soldiers in poverty. In many places war had exhausted or interrupted the supply of common, but essential, items. Templeton had become acquainted with one such case of a local woman who was in dire need of yarn for clothing. He wrote his mother: "There is a lady who got me to write to you if there could be any yarn got in that part of the country. If there can be, write to me and let me know the price. She wants to save the money and get you to send her some yarn if you have a chance. You will please answer this immediately. She says her and her Negroes are all about to get naked."

SABINA'S CIVIL WAR MEMORIES

In 1925, Mrs. Junius Little, the former Elizabeth Sabina McKenzie, published a booklet entitled *Some Memories of the Civil War: 1861–1865* in which she reminisced growing up in the Bethel community during the Civil War. She recalled:

> *Our fathers and brothers volunteered and soon were turned into companies, before being ordered from home they were trained at home, by officers elected from their different companies.* [During training sessions on drill or mustering fields], *all the women and children would go to see them muster, as we called it then. We did feel proud then to see them in their gray uniforms; but soon in April 1861, they were called to leave us, and then we realized what war was.*

When our soldiers left home the neighbors organized themselves and made a list to go to Yorkville every day, one at a time. They subscribed for a daily paper published in Columbia. Each one was ready to go when their time came, and every afternoon they would gather to wait for the mail. The carrier would wait in Yorkville for the train to come from Columbia to bring the papers. There was always someone to read it to the others…Thus it went on for four years until there were only old men and little boys to go after the mail. Generally, it was very late when they would get home, but the people would wait, and many a time we would not get any supper. After a battle the feeling would be intense. The reader probably would read the name of some of our boys killed or wounded; and so many times the news would come of someone dying of sickness. I remember well how old Mr. Quinn, our nearest neighbor, stayed until eleven o'clock one night. The mail did not come, so he went home. Later it came with a letter for him. As soon next morning as we could see, mother made me run over with it. They had just got up. Miss Jane opened it and began to read. It was to inform them of the death of their son. I never will forget it, with me a little barefoot girl, and the only one to let others know, but such was to be the lot of many others.

Everything got worse. We could not buy anything, and had to make everything at home. We could not get sugar or coffee. We made molasses in iron kettles, and that was our sweetening. We made our coffee out of parched rye, wheat, or sweet potatoes…We had to make everything we wore. We carded, spun and wove. There were two factories in Gaston where we could get yarn that we called the chain, but we carded and spun the filling. We could also get brown sheeting there, of which we made our sheets, pillowcases, our men's shirts, and our own underclothes. The wool we used we got from our own sheep. Every family had a flock of sheep. There was a carding machine down on Crowder's Creek where we got our wool carded in long rolls. We spun it on big wheels. The cotton we carded ourselves and spun on little wheels. Then we wove it on handlooms. We used to have cardings in the afternoons. One of us would ask in the neighbors and they would bring their cards and we would card all afternoon and pile all our rolls on a bed. Then the hostess would give us supper and we would go home.

We could tan the hides of our cows, sheep and goats, and we had a shoemaker to make all our shoes. If we got a calf skin for shoes, we kept those for Sunday. We also made our own hats. We platted rye or wheat straw and then made the hat out of that. When our soldiers were in Charleston, they sent us palmetto leaves, and we had fine hats then. We had all kinds of dresses. We dyed yarn with barks from the trees. The dye was set with copperas to keep it from fading. Sometimes we would get indigo, which made blue dye.

There were not many really poor people then, very few renters, so no one suffered, as we had plenty of wheat, cornmeal and such, but no money. The Negroes were most faithful, and worked the farms the same as they did when the men were at home. I could go on and on…but I am tired now, and Father Watson is gone, the post office is gone, and only the Yorkville Enquirer *and myself are left.*

DETERMINED TO FIGHT THE YANKEES

John T. Scoggins, who lived in the vicinity of King's Mountain, serves as an example of youthful patriotism that was exhibited toward the Southern cause at the outbreak of the Civil War. In April 1864, at the age of sixteen, he ran away from home, lied about his age and enlisted into the Fifth South Carolina Regiment. He was sent to Virginia, arriving in time to participate in the battles of the Wilderness, Spotsylvania and Cold Harbor. His mother reported he was underage and in the later part of August, he was declared "illegally enrolled" and sent home. Within a few months he became seventeen, and in December he enlisted into the Third Battalion of the South Carolina Reserves, which was sent to guard a prison stockade at Florence. When Sherman advanced into the state he was transferred to the command of General Joseph E. Johnston at Smithfield, North Carolina. Soon after his arrival he was stricken with pneumonia and was sent to Greensboro, where he remained until Lee's surrender. When John returned home his body was weakened by pneumonia and he never fully recovered. He died ten years later.

Next page: John T. Scoggins. *Courtesy of the Museum of Western York County.*

PRESIDENT DAVIS IN YORKVILLE AND BEYOND

As Confederate President Jefferson Davis made his way southward from Richmond with hopes of reorganizing an army in Mississippi, he passed through North Carolina, arriving in York County on April 26, 1865. That night was spent at Springfield Plantation with Colonel Andrew Baxter Springs. The next morning the entourage reassembled and headed to Yorkville.

The townspeople made ready to give the president a grand welcome. Word was incorrectly received that he would be wearing a disguise, but he was smartly attired in a plain gray suit and wore a broad brimmed hat. The bedraggled remnants of Holcomb's Legion were given the honor of leading the entourage into Yorkville. The former glory of this outfit was hidden among dirty and tattered uniforms, half-starved men and battle-scarred horses.

Among this company of Holcomb's Legion rode prankster Adolphus E. Fant of Union County. Hearing the people were expecting their leader in disguise, he thought this would be a good time to have a little fun. As the company made its way into the village, the street was lined with men, women and children hoping to get a glimpse of Jeff Davis. When the parade stopped in front of Ephraim Crenshaw's home, ladies bearing large bouquets of flowers, with tears trickling down their faces, rushed up to the mounted soldiers and said, "Do be so kind as to show me the president, do please point him out to us." When Fant was approached by a young lady who said, "Do show us Mr. Davis," he leaned down from his saddle, pointed and whispered, "There is the president." Fant pointed out a soldier in a dirty, ragged uniform with sleeves bearing the stripes of a corporal. He was mounted on a broken-down miserable horse. There was not a front tooth in his head and drool dampened a scraggy beard. The ladies rushed and surrounded him on every side, handing him huge bouquets while others tossed flowers at him until he was nearly covered. The corporal froze in his place as his gleeful company moved on, leaving him to the Yorkville ladies.

Davis was escorted to the home of Colonel Rufus Bratton, where crowds assembled to see and encourage their president. Bratton noted in his journal, "He appeared to be somewhat fatigued in body and depressed in spirits though easily aroused with his native fire. He caressed and spoke kindly to my four boys, Louis, John, Andral and Moultrie."

Rose's Hotel in York. *From the author's collection.*

That evening, before retiring, Pete, the butler, had a mishap with a tray of wine and whiskey he was taking to the president's room, spilling it on the bed and ruining the nightshirt laying there. Bratton sent the servant across the street to the home of widow Hackett to borrow a nightshirt belonging to her husband, who had been killed at the Battle of the Crater. The night passed without further incident and the next morning, the Davis entourage prepared to leave town. The president declined to make a speech, but General John C. Breckenridge, the secretary of war, spoke from the balcony of Rose's Hotel, telling the people of Yorkville to have courage.

The president left Yorkville Friday morning, April 28, 1865, heading to Unionville across the Broad River. Having traveled southward on the Pinckney Road, the entourage reached the small community of Blairsville before noon. The large troop of cavalry escorting Davis was directed to turn off onto the Rutherfordton Road in order to cross the Broad River at Smith's Ford while the president, his cabinet and guards continued to proceed on the Pinckney Road. They would rejoin on the west side of the river.

A few miles southward the Davis entourage stopped at a tavern about a mile from the Pinckneyville Ferry as preparations were being made for their crossing. At this same time, Mrs. Davis and her escort were twenty miles to the east in Chester. Davis took time to visit with the local folk, who had assembled in hopes of seeing and speaking to their president. As the sky began to grow cloudy, Davis and his cabinet said their goodbyes to the people of York County.

YANKEES ON THE BROAD

For many years it was believed that the only invasion into York County by the Union army took place on April 19, 1865, when a detachment of Stoneman's Cavalry advanced into the eastern portion of the county and destroyed the railroad bridge at the Nation's Ford near present-day Rock Hill. A little more than a week later a second, and larger, force of about three to four thousand of Stoneman's Cavalry crossed the Broad River into the western portion of York County at Smith's Ford. The main object of this force was to capture the Confederate President Jefferson Davis and his entourage, who were supposedly carrying the Confederate treasury, rumored to be about $12 million.

The river plantations of the Parks, Hamiltons, Osbornes and Thomsons were looted. When Dr. W.P. Thomson heard the looters were headed his way, he sent

Congress Street looking south, Yorkville, circa 1870. *Courtesy of the Museum of Western York County.*

his personal servant out to bury the family's silver. When he returned from his errand he and the doctor attempted to hide under the house. Thomson was a small man and was able to get into the lowest point, but the rotund servant had to be content with a shorter crawl. The physician was well concealed but the quaking servant was called out and forced to go with the Union troops. Family tradition relates that he was seen years later in Winston-Salem, North Carolina, where his captors had abandoned him.

By the time the news of the invasion reached Yorkville, the troops had re-crossed the river and were heading toward Limestone Springs in present-day Cherokee County. Nevertheless, a rider under a flag of truce was sent out from Yorkville with a dispatch informing the riders of Lee's surrender. The last account reported the rider had failed to make the rendezvous.

Joe Howell's Tall Tales

By the mid-1800s Joe Howell had gained a reputation for his tall tales. Once, in describing how rich the lands along Broad River were, he told his experience of putting in a cucumber patch in the river's bottomland. He prepared the land as normal and carefully planted the seeds. With his work done he mounted his horse and began to ride away. Hardly had he gotten settled onto his horse when he looked back and saw the vines emerging from the ground and spreading out. He urged his horse up the hill at full speed, but in spite of all the horse's efforts the cucumber vines overtook and entangled them so they came to a standstill. Reaching into his pocket for his knife to cut himself and the horse free, he said he found a fully-grown cucumber.

On another occasion Howell claimed that while he was employed as a wagoner for the ironworks at Cherokee Ford, he drove a team of mules that was so powerful they could pull eleven thousand pounds to the top of a tall hill. He said that the lead mule was so strong, when he stopped midway up the hill to give the team a rest, she would reach out and take a bush in her teeth to keep the wagon from rolling backwards. He liked to tell about the day he exchanged the trace chains for rawhide and was caught in a rainstorm. The wagon was heavily loaded and sitting atop one of the mules he encouraged this team with a lot of whooping and hollering to get them to pull the wagon to the top of a steep hill. Once he arrived on the crest, he looked back but the wagon was nowhere in sight. He explained, saying that when the rawhide harness got wet it stretched, leaving the wagon at the foot of the hill. With nothing to be done during the drenching rain, Howell said he dismounted, tied the harness to a tree on the roadside and he and the mules went home. The next day the sun came out in its full glory. When he got back to the wagon with the mules he discovered that as the rawhide traces dried they drew the loaded wagon to the top of the hill.

Hugh Hicklin "Dock" Sherer. *Courtesy of the Museum of Western York County.*

THE LAST CONFEDERATE

During the early part of January 1872, forty-nine men charged and sentenced for involvement in the Ku Klux Klan were boarded onto a Charleston-bound train in Columbia under the eye of a military guard from the Eighteenth Infantry. Among these prisoners was twenty-six-year-old Hugh Hicklin "Dock" Sherer of the Blairsville community, who would later bear the distinction of being the last surviving Confederate from the western portion of the county.

Upon arrival in Charleston the prisoners were divided and twenty-four, including Sherer and some of his neighbors, were marched from the depot under guard of a detachment of the Third Artillery, down Meeting and Broad Streets to the docks. Sentenced to eighteen months imprisonment at the Albany Penitentiary in New York State, the men were shuffled aboard the steamship *Charleston*. These York County men, many of them kin and neighbors, were described by a reporter as being a sad, forlorn lot. He wrote: "Many were imperfectly clothed, some had gaping shoes, and their persons and clothing seemed to have declared eternal war with such domestic appliances as soap and water."

At Albany the majority of prisoners were assigned to work in the shoe shop that was owned by the Eastern New York Shoe Company. Hugh and three of his brothers—James, William and Sylvanus—were four of the many assigned to this labor. Hugh's task was to cut out heels. Prison life he said was "pretty tough. For one thing the fare was very poor—sour Irish potatoes for dinner and mush and molasses for supper. But we managed to live, and that is about all you can expect to do in prison."

After serving seventeen months of his eighteen-month sentence, Hugh Sherer returned to his home in Blairsville, to his family and farm and began living a life of relative peace. The veteran lived to a ripe old age of ninety-four. In April 1939 at a birthday celebration he reflected on the times and said, "The old times were the best; people lived more sensibly then. There is a lot of foolishness now." When asked, he attributed his longevity to temperate habits. He claimed never to have been addicted to "strong drink" and while he enjoyed chewing tobacco, he did not consider himself to be a "heavy user of the weed." Though he always rose early and ate a hearty breakfast, he believed he was moderate in his eating habits.

When Dock Sherer died in October 1940, he was the last Confederate veteran living in western York County. James Ernest Lowry of York was the county's last surviving Confederate veteran. Sherer's fellow soldier died five years later in August 1945.

William Beatty Smith of Clover. *Courtesy of the Museum of Western York County.*

THE BEST BEARD IN YORK COUNTY

William Beatty Smith, born in 1840, was destined to be the father of the town of Clover and to have the longest and best beard in the county. At the outbreak of the Civil War, William enlisted as a private in the Jasper Light Infantry along with his brothers, John and Robert. Like so many Southerners, Smith believed the war would be short-lived, and vowed never to shave again until the South was victorious.

After serving a while on the coast of South Carolina, William was transferred to Virginia, where he saw his first action at the Battle of First Manassas. Eventually he was promoted to first lieutenant of Company G of the Palmetto Sharpshooters, and saw action in many of the war's most famous battles. At the battle of Seven Pines more than half of his company was either killed or wounded, including its captain. Given a captain's commission, he led his company in the battle of Frayer's Farm, the Chickahominy Campaign and the battles of Boonsboro, Sharpsburg and Fredericksburg. In the fall of 1863, he went with Longstreet to Georgia and Tennessee and fought in the Knoxville Campaign. Returning to Virginia, he fought in the Battle of the Wilderness, Spotsylvania Courthouse and Cold Harbor, Petersburg and was at Appomattox Courthouse when the conflict ended.

William returned to his home in York County after the war and became a successful planter. In 1876 he opened a mercantile business near the new Chester and Lenoir Railroad. In 1889 he formed a partnership with some other businessmen and organized the Clover Cotton Manufacturing Company. All these years he never reneged on his vow and grew the longest and most luxurious beard in the entire county. Through the years his wife would plait his glorious mane on Monday mornings and tuck it under his shirt for the week. On Sundays, she brushed and groomed his beard for church services. This they did until William's death in 1909.

WONDER HORSES

John Larue Sherer of the Blairsville community developed a seventeen-year relationship with his horse, Rawton. According to Sherer, Rawton was born on his farm in Blairsville on April 4, 1861. Five years later, on June 30, 1866, he and Sherer began carrying the United States mail and continued for the next twenty-seven years. For the rest of his life, Rawton carried his 150-pound owner and 40 to 50 pounds of mail forty miles, five days a week. Rawton died on April 25, 1879, at the age of eighteen years and twenty-one days, after only two days of sickness. Sherer would later say that Rawton was a real wonder; he "was never known to fall...nor be sick one minute in his life until his death."

Colonel Sam Jefferies had a wonder horse of his own. Though Jefferies was not from York County, but lived just across the river in Union County, he had many dealings with family and businessmen within York and western York County. In fact, he sold stud services to a number of men in York. Jefferies wonder horse, Caesar, was said to be one of the best pacers in South Carolina. Stories were told of an occasion when Jefferies mounted Caesar just as a train left the Unionville Depot. The dirt road Jefferies took crossed the railroad five times between Unionville and Jonesville—a distance of about twelve miles. By the time the train pulled into the station, Jefferies was standing on the depot platform.

During Reconstruction when the politically motivated Ku Klux Klan ruled the state, Jefferies fled safely away from arresting troops on a number of occasions. Astride Caesar he easily out-distanced his pursuers as a fox from a pack of arthritic hounds. For years after the Civil War the colonel ran boats on the Broad River. Caesar and his rider often plunged into the Lockhart Shoals to pilot a boat through the rapids. Had the wonder horse been given the power of speech, Caesar might have said, "I came, I saw, I conquered."

BUTTERMILK WALLACE

Prior to the Reconstruction era, Congressman Alexander S. Wallace of York County was one of the most respected Democrat leaders in the county and possibly the state. However, when he switched parties after the Civil War and became a supporter of Reconstruction, he became one of the county's most hated. Wallace provoked his constituents to white-hot anger when he induced President Grant to place the county under martial law. On the streets of Yorkville he was taunted and booed by white adults and tormented by hooting children. This hatred was so prone to violence that it drove the congressman from his York home, all but making him a refugee in Washington.

Conservative Democrats had such distain for Wallace that they devised the nickname "Ass" Wallace, derived from his initials, A.S. Wallace also acquired another nickname from an incident that occurred during a Congressional subcommittee's visit to Yorkville. While dining at Rose's Hotel with several members of that committee on the evening of their arrival, Major J.H. Berry picked up a pitcher of milk and threw it at the congressman. The hotel's owner interfered with Berry's throw and most of the milk fell on Representative Stevenson of Ohio. The incident nearly caused a shoot-out and riot and so infuriated and embarrassed Wallace that he used his influence in Washington to suspend habeas corpus in York County. Although Berry was arrested for assault and battery, he became a local hero among Democrats. From that point on, the congressman was known as "Buttermilk Wallace."

THE LAST GRAND STAND

What was to be termed as "the last grand stand of the Republicans in York County" took place on September 25, 1876, at Wilson's Chapel, an African American church near the tiny community of Blairsville. This meeting earned its title from an 1876 joint stump meeting between county Republicans and Democrats. About four hundred people attended this meeting, which was divided equally by race. The leaders of both parties agreed to a set of ground rules in which they agreed all political banners must be furled, a time limit was placed on each speaker and they decided who would begin and end the speeches.

Democrat Isaac D. Witherspoon of Yorkville, who had served as a captain in the Civil War, opened the speeches. Witherspoon was appreciated by both blacks and whites for his honest and fair dealings. Speaking to the blacks, he began by thanking "the colored man" for his conduct during the war while the white man was away from their homes; he claimed to personally owe their race a great debt of gratitude that he would like to repay. Hoping to defuse the

Isaac Donnom Witherspoon. *Courtesy of the Museum of Western York County.*

Ghostly Secrets, Daredevil Preachers and Walking on Water

Republican argument that white Democrats could not be trusted, he argued that the white man was not the enemy of the black man. In an apologetic tone he confessed that the Black Code had been a terrible mistake; that it had been formed "under the peculiar circumstances of the situation, thought to be for the best, but it had proved to be for the worst."

Next to speak was John Hannibal White, a black Republican congressman from Yorkville. White warned his black hearers that if Democrats were elected they would change the state constitution to nullify their civil rights. He further warned that should the Democrats gain the majority of both Houses of the Congress, they would "declare the amendments to the Constitution and the Reconstruction Acts null and void" and a bloody war would ensue.

He characterized the white legislature immediately following the war as being "onerous to the colored race" and declared that Democrats could not show a single case of legislation they had ever enacted that favored the black man. White refuted Witherspoon's remarks that the existing legislative body had brought about higher taxes, claiming they were no higher then before the war. White closed by urging the black people to "stand true" to the Republican Party as their mission of full freedom had not fully been realized.

Following Witherspoon's lead, Major Hart hailed the peaceful gathering of the two races as the wisdom of Providence that offered an opportunity to "work out our destinies together." Hart cited that it was the whites in South Carolina that passed the first law granting emancipation to slaves in August 1865, and that it was a convention of white men that approved the fourteenth amendment. He did not bother to mention that both acts were signed under threats from the federal government of being denied entrance into the Union.

Hart patronized his black audience, saying the Black Code had been "seen to be a mistake." Denying any responsibility of intent, he contended that it was of no real consequence since it had never been put into effect and there were no results of suffering. To entangle Republicans in the code, he mentioned that Congressional Representative Wallace and other prominent Republicans had voted for parts of it. But, he added, he was sure they "did it honestly." In summation, Hart compared the Republican with the Democratic ticket, saying the latter was made up of men who were pure and honest and unlike the former who, if they themselves had not stolen, had stood silently by while others did.

Representative Wallace was the last to speak and excused himself with only a few remarks. He was optimistic about the approaching election, saying he would "bottle and cork" his opponent. He encouraged the blacks to continue with the Republican Party, as much had to be accomplished to defend "the liberties of the colored people."

Wallace brought the meeting to an end, noting that "nothing having occurred to mar the proceedings [and] the most friendly spirit" of the day. As hypocritical and patronizing as these speeches may seem, they were electric and, as the election would later show, effective. The subsequent November election brought overwhelming victory for the Democrats and proved the September stump meeting was truly the last grand stand of the Republicans.

GEORGE'S CHALLENGE

Because of a lack of preachers to fill the pulpits of country churches, it was necessary for most ministers to preach a morning service at one church and a second later in the day to another congregation. During the late 1880s, Philadelphia Methodist Church south of York held its worship services at two o'clock in the afternoon, allowing its pastor time to travel from his earlier engagement.

One morning before the afternoon worship service twenty-year-old George Brown visited some of his neighborhood friends before proceeding on to the church. George was strong and tanned from his work on the family farm and stuck a striking pose on his white stallion. George's friends knew him as a daredevil, and thoroughly enjoyed dreaming up challenges that he was duty-bound to meet. On that particular Sunday the friends dared George to ride his horse through the church front door, down the aisle of the sanctuary and out the rear door. On into the early afternoon the young men had fun daring George and guessing the consequences.

When they arrived at the church that afternoon the service was already in progress and a hymn was wafting out the open windows. George was fit for the challenge. He spurred his stallion up the steps of the church, pranced down the aisle and out the back, to the utter shock of the women, stern stares of the elders and outrage of the preacher. George received many congratulations from his friends, but a stern upbraiding from his parents. A few nights later George received a second challenge, this time from the local Ku Klux Klan: do it again and he could expect a less friendly visit from them. The challenge went untaken.

THE MURDER OF
ELLISON SANDERS

K illed for his Democratic Principles." Thus reads the inscription on the small white marble slab that stands over the grave of Ellison Sanders. Ellison was born in 1862 into the African American family of Samson and Adeline Sanders. He probably had no memories of his own during the three years he spent in slavery. Some of the family believed Ellison was more fortunate than most of his emancipated race, since his family had been house servants, had been educated in crafts and obtained land soon after they gained their freedom. The family seemed to have remained in close association with their former masters, even sharing political views. This association may have, in fact, been the root cause of Ellison's death.

In 1884 Ellison became twenty-one and was anticipating voting in the November election. Like many youth, he was idealistic, and was not timid in saying he planned to vote the Democratic ticket. Political fever was running high and Bullock's Creek precinct, one of the county's most crucial, had registered 243 whites and 246 blacks.

Giles Good, a ne'er-do-well ex-slave, ever bent on violence, had aligned himself with the Republican Party from the time of emancipation. Giles was unhappy with Ellison's political leaning and took it upon himself to convert the younger man to his party. When Ellison refused to change parties, Good flew into a rage and physically assaulted him. Several days later, Ellison took out a warrant for Good, who was soon arrested. While sitting in the York County Jail, Good planned revenge though a cohort, Columbus Cranford. "Lum" was as evil as his leader and was more than willing to hear any plan against Sanders.

On Sunday, October 5, just a month before the election, Cranford hid himself in a thicket near the road leading from Chester County into the Bullock's Creek Township. Sometime between nine and ten o'clock that evening Ellison Sanders and three of his friends came up the bright, moonlit road from a church meeting when a shot rang out and Sanders fell dead. All evidence pointed to Cranford, and the following day he was arrested.

Cranford was arraigned for murder on November 1 and the trial began as soon as a jury was drawn. Cranford maintained his innocence; claiming another black man, Wallace Reed, was the killer. Supposedly Reed was organizing a group of thirty or more to kill every black man who voted the Democratic ticket. The trial ended the following day with a verdict of guilty

Grave of Ellison Sanders. *From the author's collection.*

"Big Day" at Blue Branch Presbyterian Church. *From the author's collection.*

against Cranford. Judge Cothan sentenced Sander's murderer to be hanged on December 19, but through the pleadings of Major Hart, Cranford's defense attorney, the governor granted a respite. The sentence was rescheduled for April 11, 1885.

That Friday morning, Cranford could not avoid hearing the construction of the gallows on the same floor of the jail as his cell. A number of friends and family members came to visit the prisoner, as well as his lawyer and a newspaper reporter. "I can say to you now, the first person I have told," said Cranford, "I am guilty of the crime; I fired the gun that killed Ellison Sanders." At 11:15 the sheriff came in and led his prisoner into the room where the empty gallows was waiting. Without wavering, Cranford mounted the steps and was told that he may speak to those assembled. He turned to the sheriff and recalled that the sheriff had once told him he never wanted to believe that he had hanged an innocent man; Cranford said, "You are not hanging one innocent of the charge. I am guilty of the charge." With that he said nothing more, but to thank the sheriff for his kind treatment.

A hymn was sung and Reverend Scipio Green offered a prayer. The hands and feet of Cranford were bound and his head was covered with a black cap. The noose was adjusted and at 11:26 the trapdoor cord was cut. For thirty-three minutes the body hung in suspension. Doctor Lindsay, the county physician, pronounced him dead. The body was taken down, placed in a coffin and handed over to his awaiting family.

Six months earlier the body of twenty-one-year-old Ellison Sanders had been laid to rest in the cemetery of the Blue Branch Presbyterian Church. A number of whites from the area surrounded his grave with his family and members of the black community. A short time later, the whites created a fund to purchase a stone to mark the young Democrat's grave. Today, a small white marble stone marks the site of Ellison's grave. The last line reads: "Raised by his white friends."

THE GREAT FREEZE OF 1886

John Joseph Jefferson Robinson recalled a great freeze that occurred in the Broad River area in 1886 as being the worst in his memory. According to "Three Js," the February freeze wiped out the bluebird population.

> There were lots of bluebirds in this country then. They were almost as plentiful during the winter as the English sparrows are now [but] it was several years after that winter before I again saw a bluebird…Well, it was dreadfully cold from the middle of January, as I recollect, on into March, and there was but little to do for the greater part of the time except to stay about the house and look to the firewood. Also we had to draw water for the stock, for the springs and branches were all frozen. The [Broad] River froze from bank to bank and the ice got thicker and thicker. Bateaux went out of use, and people who had business on the opposite side of the river went across on the ice.
>
> When the breakup came, an ice gang [dam] was familiar in a bend a short distance below our house and the river was backed up for nearly a mile. The ice was piled up like a little mountain. People came from all about to look at it. When the ice began to break, it made a noise like the falling of forest pines and the like. Just how thick the ice was at the thickest I do not know, but after the breakup, I measured eleven inches thick.

Dr. Rufus Bratton in Masonic regalia. *Courtesy of the Museum of Western York County.*

DOCTOR BRATTON'S CLOSE CALL

Early in the day of July 1, 1886, Dr. Rufus Bratton crossed the bridge on Bullock's Creek to call on Theodore Moore, who lived on Howell's Ferry Road. Finding his elderly patient needing constant treatment, he decided to take the old man to a family member back across the creek. While the doctor was on the west side of the creek a flash flood had occurred, swelling the waters until the bridge was entirely submerged by swift water. Pausing long enough to get some bearing on the location of the bridge, Dr. Bratton gingerly approached and passed through the water without mishap. Just as they cleared the bridge, but while still in deep water, the horse became excited and pulled the buggy and its passengers up an embankment. The buggy overturned, throwing both men into the swift current. Bratton, thinking the horse would pull the vehicle out, turned all his attention on saving his patient. The doctor was successful but the horse, in his excitement, broke the shafts of the buggy and became entangled in the harness and drowned. Wet and bedraggled, Bratton and Moore climbed onto the bank safe and alive. The horse, buggy, medical bag and all medicines were lost.

A MIGHTY PRAYER

In decades past, the flow of liquor from western York County was matched only by its great waterways. Before temperance leagues and Prohibition disrupted the flow, nearly every home in the area had its own still. Not only was the libation enjoyed, it was an easy way for the farmer to compensate for falling cotton prices and bad crops. The whiskey maker who gained the reputation of making the "best" enjoyed his vocation through the flow of extra money and an established clientele. During the late 1800s Elias Ramsey had earned one of the best reputations and even made deliveries to his customers.

Reverend Robert A. Ross of the Sharon Associate Reformed Presbyterian Church was a teetotaler and a "league man." From the pulpit and the street he denounced the making and consumption of alcohol as an evil that should be

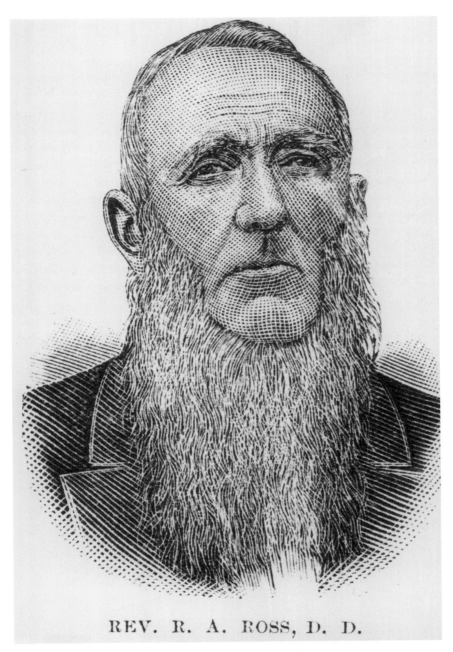

REV. R. A. ROSS, D. D.

Reverend R.A. Ross. *Courtesy of the Museum of Western York County.*

eradicated. One Sunday he went so far as to call Ramsey's operation the ruination of the community and even declared that he would pray God would send a storm to wash away the evil. The mind of both the God-fearing and the sinner reeled when word was received that a drenching rain and flash flooding had destroyed Ramsey's still.

Although Ramsey immediately began rebuilding his still, he was unnerved by the power of the old preacher to move God and the heavens. For some time Ramsey made every effort to avoid meeting the man of God by steering clear of the road that ran by the Ross home, though it created an inconvenience in making deliveries. Eventually it became necessary to take that route to York. Secretly the moonshiner hoped to ease down the road without Ross's notice, but this was not to be. As he neared the preacher's home his greatest fear was realized—Ross was in his garden by the side of the road. The situation's intensity heightened when the old man stepped out on the road and flagged him down. Ramsey braced himself for a thorough scolding. Ross was the first to speak, "Are you Mr. Ramsey?" The question was short but leading. "Yes, I am," he replied. Wanting a more positive identification, Ross questioned, "Are you the Mr. Ramsey that makes liquor?" Ramsey felt verbal cannons rolling into place. Again, Ramsey answered in the affirmative and steadied himself for the expected volley. "Well," began Ross, "wait here, my wife wants to buy a gallon." Stunned, the moonshiner did as he was told and in a few minutes Ross returned with the money and Ramsey quietly handed over a gallon of his finest. The exchange made, they bid each other good day and Ramsey rattled on down the dirt road as Ross headed to his home, jug in hand. It was not what Ramsey must have thought, however; it was later said that Mrs. Ross was often called to the bed of the sick and used the liquor for medicinal purposes and sometimes added camphor to wash the faces of corpses to keep them from turning dark before burial. No more was ever said and it is assumed the preacher and moonshiner continued in peaceful practice of their chosen vocations.

SUPERSTITIONS AND GHOSTS

As the nineteenth century drew to an end, superstition and faith were still in a struggle for the minds of many in York County. In November of 1889, African American minister Reverend E.M. Pinckney called together a mass meeting in Yorkville of black Methodists to make a statement against the practice of "conjuration." Pinckney alleged that certain individuals were taking "advantage of a large class of the ignorant [by] this accursed thing condemned by Scripture."

Pinckney and his fellow Methodists condemned the casting of spells and enchantments as a wicked practice, and regarded it as "a relic of barbarism unfit for appreciation in this the nineteenth century." They further declared that it was "a work in which no Christian could righteously engage," and they requested the intelligent people of York County's help in suppressing "this damnable blot upon our civilization."

African Americans were not the only ones in York County dealing in superstition and conjuring. Many whites continued to hold superstitious beliefs and feared witchcraft. One such account is handed down through the Moss family of western York County.

"Walking John" Moss was renowned in the area for being able to walk great distances in quickstep. One narrative tells that he hoisted a spinning wheel upon his back, walked to Union, sold the spinning wheel and was back home before dark, walking nearly fifty miles in total.

About 1890, Walking John developed some kind of affliction in his upper thigh that prevented him from walking for long periods of time. The affliction, it seems, manifested itself in a discoloration in the shape of a lizard. Unable to explain this sudden crippling ailment, John came to believe he had fallen under the spell of a witch who had put a lizard in his leg. Not getting any relief, he asked one of his sons to take him to a black woman known for her conjuring and ability to break hexes and spells. His son held to no such ideas and counted his father ignorant in his beliefs. Nevertheless, the old man continued his pleadings until the young man finally agreed to take his father to the conjuring woman.

Although the son was not a believer in witches, something happened on their way that shook the young man's faith. He told that when the two men approached a small stream and he tried to step over, his foot was pushed back by some unseen force. Time and time again he stretched his leg over the water, and each time it was pushed back. One of them came up with the idea that they had to go to the head of the stream and walk around to the other side. It worked. The trip to the conjuring woman was reported to have been successful and within a short time, Walking John Moss was back, astonishing his neighbors with his speedy travels. Though the son remained agnostic toward superstitions, he forever remembered and wondered about that day at the branch when some unseen power would not let him cross the stream.

Campaign against moonshining. *Courtesy of the Museum of Western York County.*

THE EARTHQUAKE OF 1886

During the night of August 31, 1886, parts of South Carolina were awakened by rumbling and trembling of the largest earthquake to strike the Southeast. The epicenter was located in Charleston, where 90 percent of the buildings were destroyed or damaged at an estimated cost of $6 million—the most damage since the Civil War. The quake, estimated to be 6.6 to 7.3 on the Richter scale, was felt as far away as Boston, Chicago, Alabama and Cuba. Oddly enough, some living in the Lowcountry were oblivious to its occurrence.

People living in Rock Hill and York, however, became acutely aware of a rumbling and shaking that began a few minutes before 10:00 p.m. Dishes began to rattle and then crash to the floor, heavy pieces of furniture "walked" across the room and bricks began to topple from chimneys. Many fled from their homes into the streets and roads hoping to find safety from falling timbers and flying bricks. Though the sky was clear, some screamed, "Cyclone!" As the rumblings began in York one man thought he was missing a dance next door.

Another York resident journaled that night:

> I had just laid down a few minutes when the house began to shake. It grew harder. I said to my wife, "That is a earthquake!" Getting out of bed I went to Pa's room and asked him was it an earthquake. He replied, "Yes, is it not horrible?" I answered, "Had not we better get up and be getting out of the house?" I came in our room. As I got in the passage from his room I heard a dish fall and break in the dining room. I think the first shock I heard lasted ten minutes. It may not have been so long. A second one of a few seconds came on in twenty minutes, and a very light one since I have been writing, this one twenty minutes from the second.

The more religious of the community, fearing the world was coming to an end, called upon God, vowing to live more righteously in the future. In January, Elder Parley P. Bingham of the Mormon church arrived in York County as a missionary. Protestants of the area were highly incensed by the Mormon presence and from time to time had tried to drive them away. Bingham wrote in his diary about the effects of the earthquake on the minds of local Protestants: "Some said it was the judgments of the Lord upon them for allowing the Mormons to stay in their midst, but others looking at it from a different angle said that if the Mormons had power to cause such a thing as that it would be better to do as the Mormons say."

The 1886 earthquake was caused by an accumulation of tectonic strain on the Blake Fracture Zone that occurs about every five hundred years. What was called subterranean thundering was heard later in the year; in fact, three hundred aftershocks from this earthquake were recorded during the next thirty-five years. Other than an occasional shimmer and boom York County now rests comfortably.

THE GANDER THAT DID NOT FLY

In the early 1890s the town of Yorkville was completing a standpipe that would serve as the town's new public water supply. At the time, a man known as "Professor Gander" lived within the village. It is not presently known if his friends gave this Gander his title or if he was a teacher in one of the several Yorkville schools. Professor Gander was something of a character, and when the standpipe was nearly finished, he vowed he would jump off the top to celebrate its completion.

Word that Gander was going to jump from the reservoir spread like lightning and people from all over the county made plans to be in Yorkville on the day he was to perform his death-defying plunge. This was no small feat for those living in western York County, eighteen miles from the courthouse. In those days many made the trip only once or twice a year, since a round trip might begin early in the morning and end late at night. Regardless of the distance, the streets of Yorkville were filled with spectators and thrill seekers. The more curious, who wanted to witness what was sure to be the gruesome death of the man, crowded as close to the standpipe as possible.

For some time the great crowd stood about the standpipe chatting with one another, glancing toward the top of the steel structure for a sign of any movement. As the afternoon continued, there was suddenly some commotion at the top, and the crowd fell silent. Without any fanfare, something dark leaped from the reservoir. In an instant everyone knew something was not right; it wasn't Gander—it spread wings—it was a big turkey. As the gobbler made its peaceful descent before the astonished audience they soon realized they had been the victims of a joke. The crowd was in an ill mood when the jokesters explained that they could not find the Gander, so they substituted a gobbler.

JAMES KIRKPATRICK

A fter the fall of Charleston, Tory terrorism was a constant threat to those living in the South Carolina Upcountry. In January 1781, one of the saddest stories of the era played out in the James Kirkpatrick family. James, his wife Susanna and their four sons eked out a living and lived in peace until war with Britain threatened their lives. When local militias were formed James, like his neighbors, rallied in the fight for freedom. After serving for some time without seeing his family he took leave and headed home for a short visit. On

Dr. Joseph Saye.
Courtesy of the
Museum of Western
York County.

January 1 he successfully slipped through the Tory lines and that evening James and his family sat before the fireplace. Playfully, James went over to Susannah and sat on her lap. Caught up in the joyous reunion, they were unaware that a band of Tories had surrounded the house. Suddenly the door slammed open and in an instant murderous Tories were standing in the cabin. Shots rang out before any of the Kirkpatrick family could move and in the same moment James Kirkpatrick fell dead from his wife's lap. This tragedy gave the young husband and father the dubious distinction of becoming the first war casualty and third person to be buried in the Bullock's Creek Presbyterian Cemetery.

NEVER A SQUAWK

I n the early days of York County, the country doctor was sometimes called upon to perform dentistry. Dr. Joseph Saye, Sharon's first physician, liked to tell about such a call when, as he said, he was a young and foolish practitioner. He told he had been called to pull a tooth for a young woman who had been suffering from an abscessed molar for several days.

Her face was swollen until it resembled a full moon. I got the tooth out; but not until she had squalled so long and loud that she could be heard a mile in each direction. She had a brother who did not have any more sense than the law allowed and who witnessed the operation. He chided her about crying and being a baby and all that sort of thing and finally he concluded, "Why sister, I'll let the doctor pull out any tooth I have in my head and I'll bet you he can't make me holler." The sister insisted that he would yell too, and she insisted that he be put to the test. And I was not loath to do the thing because I believed he would yell and besides as I said, I was just naturally devilish in those days. So he opened his mouth and I never saw whiter, firmer, prettier teeth in my life. I clamped down on a big molar and I twisted and turned. Finally it came out—a big fellow with four roots and as perfect as could be. But sure enough, there was never a squawk out of him!

You're the First Fool to Come Along

Joe Logan was a well-educated man and a superb teacher. He had one fault that seemed to totally rule his life: he generally tarried too long at the jug. He was often heard to say, "One good swallow is worth two sets of teeth." Even when he was not inebriated he had a peculiar speech impediment that sounded like, "Ye shee shir, I'm Joe Logan and hish a schmart old animal!"

After one of his numerous drinking bouts, on the way home he became tired and laid down in the road to sleep it off. Chess McKinney came along and warned him, "Uncle Joe, some fool is apt to come along and run over you." Logan turned toward the merchant and said, "Mishter McKinney, you shir is the first fool to come along and you hadn't done it!"

Dem Bones Dem Dry Bones

Not long after Dr. Joseph Saye came to Sharon to begin his medical practice as a young man, he became desirous of a skeleton to place in his office either for study or ambiance. After some time had passed, a man was hanged in York for murder and was buried in a field outside town. Under the cover of darkness, Doctor Saye and a black assistant went to the gravesite and exhumed the body. The body was placed in Saye's wagon and was brought to the doctor's home in Sharon. The next day the two men built a fire around a large iron pot filled with water. They placed the corpse in the boiling water to remove the flesh from the skeleton. The black man was left in charge of the operation and every so often Saye would come by to see how the job was progressing. On one of his rounds he found the black man adding wood to the fire and singing to himself:

You bad nigger—kill the white man
Dat why you biling in de pot.

It may have been that Doctor Saye took his cues from Dr. Rufus Bratton on how to acquire a skeleton, since he, too, had acquired a skeleton in a very similar way. The story begins on the morning of September 10, 1852, when the marital relationship between two Cleveland County residents, George and Mary Langford, turned ugly. Their marriage had taken a rocky road years earlier, paved with jealousy. George was described as polite and tasteful in his manners and dress and he kept his boots neatly blackened—some may take this description as merely a comment on his meticulous ways while others suspect he was a "ladies' man." Whatever the reason, Mary grew extremely jealous of her husband and gradually became hateful to him. Feelings had become so strained between the two that they refused to take their meals at the same table.

Near ten o'clock that fateful morning, Mary returned from an overnight visit with a married daughter and was met by her husband. An argument quickly ensued and George, driven to white-hot anger, choked his wife to death. As her body fell into a corner of a rail fence, the top rail tumbled and fell and landed across her neck and shoulders and legs. George claimed Mary had taken a fall from the rail fence, but when Doctor Williams of Shelby performed an autopsy, he found her windpipe had been compressed. On her neck he discovered the impression of a thumb and three fingers.

George was arrested and convicted of murder. Following an appeal to the North Carolina Supreme Court, which sustained the verdict, George Langford was hanged just west of the town of Lincolnton. Knowing that graves of criminals were often robbed, Langford had previously arranged to have a man guard his grave for some time, paying him ten dollars a month. Doctor Bratton apparently made a better deal. For an undisclosed amount of money the black man agreed to exhume Langford's body, strip it of all its clothing and bring it to Bratton's York County plantation. There, Bratton eviscerated the body and boiled the flesh from the bones. Tradition has it that on one occasion the skeleton was paraded in the streets of York. After that it disappeared from sight, though some claimed they saw it during the mid-1900s.

I Got Home Before the Dogs

It's been told that there was a patch of woods near Hickory Grove once owned by a man by the name of Traylor who hanged himself there. Many believed the spirit of the dead man haunted those woods. Supposedly the forest had an abundant supply of possums, much desired by the poor for their supper table. One reason for so many possums within those woods was that the animals could not be successfully hunted during daylight hours, and there were very few who would hunt those woods because of reports of the ghost. Most men totally avoided the area and even the bravest heart that entered the woods was a bit skittish.

The only account of a sighting of the ghost was told by an anonymous hunter who told of his one and only experience in the Traylor woods. It went like this:

Before I got very far into the woods the dogs treed. I looked up and thought I saw a possum. Switching the light behind my back I commenced trying to shine his eyes. Before I knew it the possum kept getting bigger and higher until all at once it looked to me like a full-grown man standing on a limb. I didn't do a thing but throw down my torch and lit out from there. There were two ten-rail fences between the woods and home; but all the same I got home before the dogs did.

He Can Walk on Water

About 1909 a holiness preacher by the name of Childers arrived in Sharon saying that he could walk on water. After capturing the attention of many with his preaching and his promise to prove his approval from God, a large crowd gathered at Bullock's Creek just outside town to see him walk on water. Dressed in a white flowing robe and barefoot he preached to the crowd and moved toward the rippling waters—sure enough, he treaded upon the waters that lapped hardly to his ankles!

Historic block in town of Sharon. *From the author's collection.*

Many were carried away with the miracle and believed their own eyes, but others were more skeptical and were determined to find the truth about the matter. Returning to the creek, some of the local men found a plank walkway just under the surface of the water. Seeing the so-called evangelist had duped the local people; they decided to get the best of him. They bored several holes across the plank, just enough to hold it in position but not to withstand the weight of the man. After the preacher announced he would walk on the water again, a great crowd assembled along the banks and hills of Bullock's Creek. From the waterside he preached a fiery sermon and at just the right moment stepped into the water. Suddenly the plank gave way and the preacher went headfirst into the water. A howl of rage went up from the duped crowd. Some of the sisters lunged for Childers as he came coughing and sputtering from the creek. The last time the bedraggled preacher was seen he was running down the road to Chester with an angry mob behind him.

LAZARETTO
SOUTH CAROLINA

In March 1781, a smallpox epidemic occurred along the Broad River affecting many living in what are now York, Union and Cherokee Counties. The home of Reverend Joseph Alexander, pastor of the Bullock's Creek Presbyterian Church, was converted into a hospital, thus making it the first clinic in the South Carolina Backcountry. During the epidemic Major Joseph McJunkin was stricken and his mother, Mary Ann Bogan McJunkin, came to the manse to nurse her son and others who lay ill. Although the major recovered, his mother died of smallpox in April. Due to the dispensing of inoculations many recovered, to the surprise of their families. The results of this cure were so miraculous that the Alexander home was called "Lazaretto" in reference to the Biblical account of Jesus raising Lazarus from the dead.

THE BIRTH OF A NATION

The 1915 silent movie *The Birth of a Nation* was adapted from Thomas Dixon's novel and play, *The Clansman*, which was written about the Reconstruction activities of the Ku Klux Klan in York County. While this fact is commonly known, few know that a man from York County made an important and historical contribution to D.W. Griffith's production of the provocative movie.

Author Thomas Dixon wrote Ambrose Gonzales, the publisher of *The State* newspaper, about Griffith's plans to produce a movie and his need for a Columbia contact to verify the script for accuracy and provide photographs. Gonzales assigned a young reporter by the name of Sam to the job. Sam had little knowledge of history and was unsure if he could handle the assignment. The publisher, however, encouraged him, saying it was a good opportunity to earn extra money. The assignment was easier than Sam had thought. All Dixon and Griffith needed were photographs of the chamber of the South Carolina House of Representatives.

Sam approached Columbia photographer George V. Hennies to do the work. Originally Griffith had planned to film in the State House, but when he began running over his budget, he ordered the chambers to be constructed on the movie lot using Hennies's photographs. When the job was completed, Sam received a sizeable check for his work and years later recalled with pride that Griffith noted his part in the making of *The Birth of a Nation*. Samuel L. Latimer Jr. was a son of York County, born near the Beersheba Church community, the son of Samuel Latimer, who was born in 1857.

THE PERFECTLY PROTECTED POSSUM CLUB

As the year 1919 came to a close and possum-hunting season continued, a unique hunting club and social event developed in Sharon that rivaled any affair of the year. That November a band of would-be hunters consisting of a number of young women went on a possum hunt after hearing the men and boys of Sharon tell their exciting tales of the hunt.

One nighttime excursion was enough to convince the girls that this was something they wanted to do on a regular basis. When asked about their newfound entertainment one responded, "It was great to tramp the woods and hollows on a moonlight or moonless night in December, accompanied by father or brother or 'friend,' to listen to the talking of a good possum dog, hot on the trail of the peculiar little animal that made the sweet potato famous."

The girls gained some local notoriety when the *Yorkville Enquirer* published a story on the girl's hunting expeditions. Hoping to tease the girls, a local man told them that the county game warden, D.T. Woods, was going to prosecute every one of them for not paying $1.10 apiece for a hunting license. The jokester went on to say they would be hauled "into court along side of blind tigers and burglars and profiteers and Bolsheviks." The threats got the girls all up in the air, and although no names had been mentioned in the recent newspaper article, they protested to the newspaper office and got the reporter in trouble with his editor. Hoping to eliminate any future trouble, every one of the girls purchased a hunting license, which led them to call themselves the "Perfectly Protected Possum Club."

Usually the girls' nocturnal hunting trips were lead by champion possum-hunter Walter Maloney. Not only was Maloney an expert in possum hunting, his wife was well known as the best possum cook around. On Tuesday nights the club and their friends gathered around the dinner table at the Maloney home for a feast of baked possum and sweet potatoes. (Fried chicken was offered to those who lost all interest in possum after it was caught. Rice and gravy, cakes, pickles and fruit were also on the menu.)

Eventually the dinners became so well attended that they developed into stand-up dinners. Supper guests included the huntresses, Hannah and Lucy Stephenson, Susie Hartness, Margaret Boyd, Annie Whitesides, Annie Ferguson, Daisy Anthony, Stella and Penninah Cain, Pauline Turner, Nellie Ricker, Mary Bell Good, Nannie Mae Plexico, Eunice Cain and Myrtle Henry; adult chaperones Mr. and Mrs. O.M. Spurlin, Mr. and Mrs. L.H. Good, Mr. and Mrs. W.A. Fewell; and single men E.M. Shillinglaw, Ralph and Augustus "Gus" Cain, J.B. Paysinger, Ross Ricker, James D. Grist, Brown Baird, W.T. McClain, T.D. Turner, James "Jim" Youngblood and Clyde Potts. At one of the earlier dinners, Game Warden Woods and his wife were special guests. Warden Woods was given the honor of calling all to supper and saying grace. After supper the hunters and friends were entertained by music furnished by Mrs. W.A. Fewell, Edward Shillinglaw, Mr. and Mrs. L.H. Good and Walter and Ed Maloney.

Sam Dowdle of Sharon astride a darnedest thing. *Courtesy of the Museum of Western York County.*

Hill's Gin House burning, 1910. *Courtesy of the Museum of Western York County.*

THE DARNEDEST THING

Years before racecar driver Ralph DePalma set a world record for speed in 1925 at Phoenix, Arizona (he covered five miles in 3.53 minutes), George Glenn of York County was setting a few speed records of his own. George was a daring young man with an aptitude for mechanics. The motorcycle was his vehicle of choice and it appears he was one of the first, if not the first, to own a motorcycle in western York County. He was easily recognized as a "speed demon," as he would often be seen racing over rough roads, making daring turns and maneuvers. Reminiscing some years later, Glenn said, "Well, I tell you, I rode a motorcycle for a good while and had lots of pleasure out of it. But it is a dangerous proposition. I got lots of falls and although I was never seriously hurt as a result, I finally concluded that it was most too dangerous for me and I quit. A motorcycle is the only darn thing I ever saw that would throw you off and then come back and jump on you."

THE ENGINE THAT WOULD NOT DIE

William L. Hill, one of Sharon's first entrepreneurs who deservedly earned the title "Dean of Merchants," owned and operated numerous businesses in the town that was spawned by the cotton culture of York County. During the second decade his sizeable holdings included fifteen farms in the surrounding area and within the town he owned and managed a cotton gin, car dealership, warehouses and had built a three-story department store that boosted the economy in a thirty-mile radius. The destruction of cotton gins by fire was common because of the combustibility of cotton lint that clung to every ledge and corner of the buildings. A spark could easily ignite the lint, and once it began to burn, the fire would spread with the rapidity of a gasoline blaze and was virtually impossible to extinguish. In January, just before the Depression of 1920 was felt in Sharon, a fire swept through the Hill's gin house, reducing it to ashes in less than an hour with a loss of property estimated at $10,000.

When the rubble was cleared, the fifty-horsepower Fairbanks-Morse diesel engine was found to be salvageable. Porter Good of Bullock's Creek purchased the engine and after restoring it, installed it in his gin house. Ten or fifteen years later, Good's operation burned to the ground. Again, the one-cylinder engine was retrieved from the ashes and restored. Good rebuilt his gin and installed the hardy engine. In 1947, fire destroyed that gin house, but still the engine survived. Good rebuilt the defiant engine and used it to power a sawmill. Six years later, in 1953, the day after the last piece of lumber was sawed for the new Bullock's Creek Presbyterian Church, the sawmill burned to the ground. For weeks a column of smoke rose from the smoldering pile of sawdust, yet Hill's old engine stood proudly among the ashes, having experienced four devastating fires. Time, however, had caught up with the engine and its owner—both were too old to start over. Good died the following year and the cylinder of the engine was last seen in 1963, when the site was cleaned and it was buried in a landfill.

KILLED BY LIGHTNING

While hauling hay from a field near his home about three miles south of Hickory Grove, a bolt of lighting struck thirty-year-old William A. Ramsey, his young son and both mules. Ramsey and one of the mules were instantly killed. The Ramsey boy was unhurt and the other mule was badly shocked. William Ramsey was buried the following day, September 21, 1921, leaving a widow and seven children.

Another more interesting death by lightning occurred about 1830 near Ninety-Nine Islands, when a bolt from heaven killed Willis Moss. That year crops were suffering from a long dry spell and every cloud that formed over the river was hoped to contain relief. Among the farmers who thought they might lose their crops was Willis Moss, "a very wicked, thoughtless kind of man."

One evening thunderclouds began to form across the river in Union County. Willis Moss sat in the doorway of his home with two of his children on his lap. Moss watched the clouds as they headed up and began to move toward his farm. Thunder began rumbling and rain could be seen in the distance, but before the rains reached his farm, the storm broke up and all hopes of relief were lost. Moss made some wicked remark against God and His works and before the last word of the sentence was spoken, a lightning bolt came crashing through the roof, shattered a gun hanging above the door and hurled Moss into eternity. Neither of the children sitting on his lap was hurt other than a slight shock. The baby, Barnett, who was lying in his cradle at the time, was struck in the head by a piece of the rifle and his clothing was set on fire. As soon as she recovered from the jolt, Mrs. Moss rushed to her baby's side and extinguished the fire.

THREE HATLESS MEN

After the town's second policeman, Shep Huey, resigned in 1921, the town of Sharon had difficulty keeping a law enforcement officer. In those days the town had no property taxes and Huey was paid through fines and forfeitures. He made a good living as long as the crime rate was high, but when it fell, he felt a definite pinch in his back pocket and took up a job in York.

Upon Huey's resignation, Mayor Dennis Whisonant posted the job and received eighty-seven applications. One applicant, W.A. Settlemyer, a seasoned policeman from King's Mountain, was hired. However, Settlemyer did not last long; in fact, he deserted the position within twelve hours. It was said around town that shortly after taking his position, three drunken men without hats came into town and were so fierce acting that Settlemyer turned in his handcuffs to a member of the town council and boarded the evening train for parts unknown.

Within a week or so, after his so-called cowardliness was published in the *Yorkville Enquirer*, Settlemyer came to York and had a long discussion with that newspaper's editor. He told Editor Grist that he had reported for duty on October 25. From the beginning he saw little organization. The town clerk could not find the keys to the jail or the badge and he was given "a pair of ancient handcuffs or irons which had probably done valuable service during slavery times and which any museum would be glad to pay a fancy price for." Settlemyer complained, "Thus equipped and fortified, they expected me to sally forth to cope with the forces of lawlessness and bandits of Sharon and suburbs, to be traffic cop, health officer, street foreman, town detective, besides being Vice Officer and Chief of Police, and on special occasions to furnish escorts of honor to distinguished visitors. All this for the sum of $75 per month, to board myself and family and furnish my own clothes."

Settlemyer told the editor that after studying the situation, he "thanked the honorable Mayor and Town Council for the honor they had done me in tendering me the office, with its high honors and emoluments…respectfully

Ladies Sunday school class of Mount Vernon Methodist Church, circa 1920. *Courtesy of the Museum of Western York County.*

declined the position and caught the night train." He continued, "I did not go to work, because what the Town of Sharon needs is a combination of William J. Burns, John J. Pershing, George W. Goethals, Carrie Nation, Billy Sunday and Herbert Hoover!"

HOW TO MAKE A NEW DOOR

In the early 1930s, Sharon was the home of a man who suffered from extreme depression and often spoke of ending his life, believing he had no real future. Everyone in town knew the man and his gloomy attitude and was convinced that some day he would kill himself. From one incident we know that he must have had his moments as a fun-loving comedian. One cool morning he came into the local blacksmith shop where a number of men had gathered around a large pot-bellied stove, waiting for their mules to be shod or other metal work to be completed. As usual he began to bemoan his situation, believing that day was the day he would do himself in. With little fanfare, he pulled a stick of dynamite from his pocket, jerked opened the stove door and tossed in the stick. For a split moment the men stood in shocked disbelief, and all at once every man made a mad dash for the door. Instantly the doorway was filled from jam to jam with terrified men crying out for an exit. One young farmer, seeing the exit blocked, became frantic and in a wild effort to save his life, ran through the shop wall. Safely outside and some distance away, the men silently waited for the explosion. Seconds seemed like hours before they realized something was amiss. As they cautiously approached the shop they heard hysterical laughter coming from the open door. It had only been a short stick painted red.

QUEER OLD IDEAS

In 1925 Dr. Saye recalled earlier days of his practice, saying,

Just how they came to be, unless it was because of gross ignorance, I don't know, but folk hereabouts had some queer ideas about things when first I came. And many of them in cases of sickness did not believe, or rather did not practice the belief that cleanliness is next to godliness. I recall that just after I came to this section forty years ago, I was called to attend a lady who had given birth to a child. She had been given absolutely no attention so far as bathing was concerned, and the child had not been bathed although it was twelve hours old. In the close, stuffy room where the little child had been born were seated about a dozen old women around a raging hot fire. In a bed were two children sick with measles. I gave orders that the mother and child be bathed. The old women looked at me as though I was crazy and one of them informed me that never in all that community had she heard of mother and babe being bathed and clothing changed until the baby was three days old. And do you know, I had to raise a row sure enough before I could get my order carried out: the old women shaking their heads and muttering while some of them predicted that both mother and child would surely die. It took me a good while to get that silly notion out of lots of heads.

A PROGRESSIVE FARMER

John S. Hartness was best known for his civic leadership and for his years of service as a longtime cashier-manager of the First National Bank of Sharon. Like most professional men of his time, he was a farmer as well. In 1929, he owned the old Hafner Place near Turkey Creek and on this farm he experimented with newly imported vegetation that was being touted as a good groundcover, land builder and summer grazing for cattle. The weather was extremely dry the year he began his experiment and it continued for the next two or three years and he did not get the advertised results. Hartness's expectations were soon met and then surpassed as the vine began to ramble over everything in its path. The experimental groundcover was kudzu.

IF THEY RIDE THE ELEPHANT THEY MAY NOT RIDE THE DONKEY

In 1932 the Republican Party was attempting to make a comeback in York County. Dr. Joseph Saye of Sharon was chairman of the York County Democratic Executive Committee. To insure that no closet Republican was lurking about on the Democratic Roll Books, Saye ordered that each committee member investigate everyone they knew with Republican leanings and he would purge them from the roll. "If they ride the elephant," Saye proclaimed, "they may not ride the donkey… hereafter they must confine any political participation…to the Republican camp." Saye went on to explain that "Republicans had no more right to participate in the Democrats' business, than a Presbyterian Deacon could walk in and vote to call a preacher in a Baptist congregation."

As Franklin Roosevelt's first term began drawing to an end, the Democratic political machinery cranked into motion. In 1935 the state's first all-women reelection club was formed in the village of Sharon. Mrs. James D. Grist,

A Sharon girl campaigns in 1929. *Courtesy of the Museum of Western York County.*

president of the Woman's Roosevelt for Reelection Club, led the women in a fundraiser. It was decided they would make a quilt and auction it at a special event. The ladies worked diligently to create a quilt with a red, white and blue motif with a deep red border and a lining of blue on black. In August of that year the club sponsored a picnic and rally with about one thousand people attending. John S. Rainey, a prominent businessman and father-in-law to Doctor Saye, presided over the affair and introduced each candidate with jokes and wisecracks. Western York County's ever-present beef hash, prepared by Vines Howell, R.C. Blackwell and John M. Davison, was liberally dished out to the picnickers.

Robert M. "Bob" Whitesides, a veteran auctioneer, began auctioning the Roosevelt reelection quilt. The bidding began at $35 and sputtered and halted several times. When it was announced that Mrs. Herbert B. Swope of New York, a member of the National Democratic Committee, had telegraphed a bid of $100, the bidding revived. A three-man team composed of F.M. Mellette, Sam B. Pratt and W.L. Hill Jr. made the final bid of $150 and walked off with the patriotic quilt. While the amount may seem small to us today, since the nation was in the depths of the Great Depression and little money was circulating, Mrs. Grist was pleased to contribute so much to Roosevelt's reelection coffers.

SON DOVER

Sometime in 1933, Son Dover was serving out a two-year sentence in the York County jail for robbing Whitesides's Store in Hickory Grove. Dover soon proved he could be an exemplary prisoner and he was made a trustee with the privileges of walking unguarded to and from the courthouse where he worked as a janitor. Though he was a trustee he secretly longed for more freedom and in March of 1934, he and six others escaped and fled from York County. For nearly four years Dover eluded the police, fleeing to New Orleans and to Hanford, California, where he was arrested in February 1937 and jailed for robbery under the alias Louis Johnson. When the York County Sheriff was notified and asked about expediting him to York, the sheriff said Dover was not worth the expense and if he stayed out of the county it would be counted good riddance. Son, however, longed for home and returned to York County before the year's end. When the sheriff heard he had returned and was living at his parents' home in Hickory Grove, he and Constable Frank Ramsey went to arrest him.

As it turned out, Son Dover was an expert rock thrower and when the law officials arrived at the Dover home, he set up a barrage that kept the policemen dodging for cover. During the rock bombardment Ramsey was hit and fell to the ground. Seeing his moment to escape, Dover fled on foot, but in his flight stumbled over a fifteen-foot cliff and was knocked unconscious. The sheriff awakened him by a few sharp slaps across the face and returned Dover to the York jail. Dover was retained in the county jail for only a short time, and by the summer of 1938 he was working on the Dagnall farm near Hickory Grove. That August he was seriously injured while pulling stumps with a team of mules. Some hours later, at the age of thirty-five, Son Dover's short, tragic life came to an end.

JIM CROW OF SHARON

As the political atmosphere thickened in 1938, one of the town's pets became involved in politics. Smith Cobb had a pet crow he called "Jim Crow," in dubious honor of the Jim Crow laws. Throughout the spring, Jim had been content to make visits along Woodlawn Avenue, but after August he crossed the railroad tracks and started hanging around town with the farmers and businessmen. He was fond of perching on cars in front of the post office, Caldwell's or Buck Youngblood's store. From time to time he would cross the street to a car in front of the drugstore, or the Maloney Brothers or Kennedy's Variety Store and then venture on down to Cobb's Grocery Store. After a while he would fly up to Rainey's Gin to see what was going on there and then back across the street to Ernest Dowdle's filling station.

Making his way though the business district, he would call on Brice Bigham, John Hope and Charley Gourley. Satisfying his curiosity there, he would go on to Hill & Company and then look over the new cars at Hill Motor Sales. All along the way, he would fuss and quarrel with folks who seemed to cross him the wrong way, like folks do from time to time. Taking up on one of his favorite perches he would call out to anyone who might give him the time of day. Some said he sounded like a candidate at a political picnic. During his stump campaigns he was known to grow more raucous and sometimes shout out a positive promise or two.

Jim Crow it seems was not one bit afraid of Jean Grist's cats, Nanski and Bohunkus. When he was just a fledgling the two cats pestered him on a daily basis, but since he had matured they were choosy about their association with him. But on the other hand, he was very leery of David Byers's dominecker hen since they had a dispute one day that left Jim in a huff and he no longer cared about having any dealing with the peculiar old hen. The dispute took place one morning when the hen was enjoying a juicy worm and Jim tried to take it away from her. She flew into a rage and with the fury of a regiment of Johnny Rebs, lit into him, ripping out a few feathers from the northern end of a southbound escape.

Jim, however, was a welcome sight to visitors and residents of the town, having become used to his fussing and preaching. Then, in September, Jim disappeared and was no longer seen or heard in Sharon. It was expected he answered the call of the wild given sweetly by a raven beauty with a lot of promise. One citizen, however, figured Jim Crow had gotten fed up with all the political talk and buncombe that was going around preceding the fall election.

THE LUCK OF TIZ RAINEY

John "Tiz" Rainey and his wife, both of Sharon, were seriously injured when he wrecked their A Model Ford by driving into an embankment in October 1937. Mrs. Rainey's leg was broken just below the knee and her throat was cut by glass and John was crushed by the steering wheel. After Doctor Burrus attended to their wounds, they were sent to St. Phillips Hospital in Rock Hill. This accident would have had little significance, but John was no stranger to accidents. Once he had thrown his wife out of the car while making a sudden turn, he was scalped in another automobile accident and he was also accidentally shot in the shoulder.

YOU BETTER BE LOOKIN' UP

Recalling his childhood days on his daddy's farm, Johnny B. Gilfillan in 2001 said he started plowing with a mule as soon as he got big enough to walk behind a plow. "I was running out furrows when I was just thirteen," he said matter-of-factly. During these recollections he remembered two female mules his father owned and worked in the 1940s, Rhody and Duck. "Rhody had some age on her when Daddy bought her," he said, "but she was the best dern mule as I ever got behind." Beside the mules, Johnny's father also raised and trained two bulls to pull a plow. Both of them were good workers, but one, a white-faced Hereford, worked fine until he got hot and then "he would head to the bushes! You couldn't stop him—he would pull you and the plow through the trees—you could hear the tree roots just-a poppin'!" Johnny paused for a good laugh and then said, "I was never so glad when Daddy sold those bulls to Hicks Moss!" When asked why, since they were such good workers, he said, "They were aggravatin'! When you was hookin' 'em up to a single tree, you'd better be lookin' up or they would sh—— on your head every time!"

Allen and Hanson Gardner (grandsons of the author) point to the future. *From the author's collection.*

Visit us at
www.historypress.net